Gray's Fish Cookbook
A MENU COOKBOOK

Gray's Fish Cookbook
A MENU COOKBOOK

by Rebecca Gray with Cintra Reeve

Photography by Frank Foster
Watercolors by Thomas Aquinas Daly

1986
GSJ Press
South Hamilton, Massachusetts

Library of Congress Catalog Card Number 86-83013
International Standard Book Number 0-9609842-6-7
Published by   GSJ Press
                205 Willow Street
                South Hamilton, Massachusetts 01982

Printed in the United States of America

To my most honest food critics—
Hope, Caroline, Sam, Doug, and Will Gray

Acknowledgements

It is a rare relationship in this world, a co-authorship that can last through the months it takes to write a book. It is an extraordinary thing to have it last through two books. Many, many thanks to my co-author, Cintra Reeve Rossi, who has always been a joy to work with. May there continue to be many books together.

Many thanks to Larry Taylor for his beautiful book design and fine sketches. A special thanks to Frank Foster and Pat Dunlea for their inspired creativity and technical knowledge of how to produce the best in food photography.

Thank you, thank you, Tom Daly, for the use of your fabulous paintings. Your watercolors add a lovely dimension to this book for which I am very grateful.

Thanks to Becky Petersen for hours of copy editing and to Donna Williams for proofreading, and to Holly Meade for putting it all into pages.

Thank you, too, *Gray's Sporting Journal* subscribers, for your inspiration and encouragement.

And to all who have taken part in my fishing pleasures, thank you. Finally, more than thanks to Ed Gray, my fishing partner, my editor, my mentor, my friend and most happily, my husband.

Contents

Preface

I wrote *Gray's Wild Game Cookbook* with a fair degree of confidence. There simply are not that many people in the world who hunt (know what happens afield to the animal), have access to a variety of game, have a good basis and interest in gourmet cooking and remain on friendly and intimate terms with a word processor. It was easy to be an expert and to go unchallenged about anything I wanted to write concerning game cookery.

Fish are a different story. Everyone cooks and eats fish. Everyone has an Aunt Lizzie who cooks a mean fish chowder or has a fabulous recipe for flounder or pike or snapper. Over forty million people hold fresh water fishing licenses, and how many more must there be who fish regularly in the oceans? Fishing and eating fish are older than the Bible; everyone knows about it. So how can I be so egotistical as to claim expertise and write a book about cooking fish? Everyone knows about fish.

There are many, many people who know more about cooking fish than I do. And certainly there are many, many, many people who know more about how to cook their own local fish or their own most frequently caught fish than I do. I cannot pretend to be an expert on the subject of fish cooking.

My partner in this book, Cintra Reeve, said to me one time that a good measure of a cook's true capabilities is how well she cooks a hamburger. Unfortunately, this was said after I had just thrown some burger in a fry pan absent of butter or seasoning, turned the flame on full blast and laid a rather stale, hard bun on the plate. It is hardest to cook the usual, the common and the basic. My interest rarely wavers when painting citrus leaves with chocolate to decorate a mold of white chocolate mousse, or when I must figure out a menu using Dall's sheep and porcini mushrooms. But give me my 900th bluefish to cook and it's been hard at times to fight back the yawns.

I'd like with this book to change your "usual." Certainly the reason there are so many different cookbooks and that cookbooks sell well every year is because we get a little bored with our usual recipes and just the variety any new book offers helps alleviate some of the boredom. But I'd like to impart in this book a little more than just variety; I'd like to alter the attitudes. Can I offer a change in. . . philosophy? Oddly enough, my own shift in attitude has come through the process of becoming a better fisherman and a better cook. Two different avocations both reaching for the same philosophical goal.

I am very fortunate to be able to spend two weeks each year fishing in Alaska. Each of the camps we visit has an abundance of either Dolly Varden or grayling. An "abundance" in Alaska means absolute gluttony anywhere else. It would not be uncommon or require much skill to catch 15 or 20 on a fly of either fish per day. This could lead to monotony, and for some it does. They reel the fish in too quickly hoping that lack of finesse will allow him to escape and consequently avoid spending the time bringing the fish to shore for unhooking. But for many of us the commonness of the little Dolly makes us willing to experiment. Maybe switch to some weird dry fly that the guide invented rather than continue to wave the tried-and-true Flash Fly in front of Mr. Dolly. I heard yesterday someone took a Dolly on a mouse! Let's try it! And with the catching of each fish we learn what makes them alike and familiar and what makes them unique. So many caught one after another makes it easy to begin to know his style of strike, to know his fight and know when he is tired and should be played no longer. But each has his own little personality, too. Why, a grayling that jumps and twists when hooked! He must have been taking lessons from a rainbow trout. To know the fish is to respect him. I have had more than one fishing guide who, after the fight and the fish is being released, thanks the fish for the fun he has given us. It is a habit I have found myself imitating. To become engrossed in the fun of experimentation, enjoy familiarity with the fish, to respect him is to learn also how to focus and concentrate on fishing. When three days fishing seems like lightening fast seconds passing, when the scenes from "The Old Man and the Sea" and Spencer Tracy's monologues with the fish become your reality, then you not only have become a good fisherman but found the ingredients for becoming a good cook.

Cooking is not different than fishing in this respect. The 900th bluefish may taste best grilled, but instead of serving it with tomato sauce all over it just for the sake of experimentation and variety, try making the menu more interesting. Try serving a grilled bluefish with couscous with porcini. Taking the time, having the patience, caring about the preparation of the fish is what makes the difference. I believe you very literally taste the difference in a meal when a cook has been thoughtful and focused on the food. If you learn to experiment, learn to respect the fish that you are preparing and can focus totally on the preparation you will have the greatest fun and cook the best meal.

Does it sound like I think that in order to be the best of fish cooks you also have to be the best of fishermen and vice versa? This isn't always practical. Isn't it easier to read a book? So I wrote this book, not as the expert but as someone who has spent some time staring down that line into the blueness of the water thinking about old Mr. Fish down there. And as someone who has spent time with him in the kitchen. I hope that a little bit of my imagination, respect for the fish, and desire to focus on the problem of how to cook him will make a useful book for you—and pass along a happy philosophy.

Salmon

Salmon is a wonderful fish. Whether you fish for Atlantic or Pacific salmon or pull them out of Lake Michigan, their energy and excitement in the water are unmistakable. A beautiful, flavorful fish that lends itself to many varied recipes, he is surely as interesting and fun in the kitchen as in the water. Except when he is to be poached.

On a trip several years ago to Labrador we were lucky enough to bring home twelve beautiful Atlantic salmon. Obviously recipe versatility was called for, poaching being one of the clear and desirable choices. I learned quickly that you should always release the salmon that are over the size of 24 inches if you intend to poach them. In all of North America (and probably Europe, too) there does not exist a poacher large enough for any salmon I've had the pleasure of meeting. I know this for a fact since I called every kitchen store in the world looking for a poacher over the size of 24 inches. Many of the recipes I found in my cookbooks called for poaching large salmon in the dishwasher(?!) This being too bizarre I spoke with my professional friends. First, I talked with our French-Canadian publisher friend—a great fisherman, and the person who had accompanied us to Labrador. He had gotten his poacher by welding together two stainless sausage containers found in a remote meatpacking house in northern Quebec. This was not too helpful. I then spoke with my cooking friends who referred me to restaurant supply houses in East Boston, but who suggested that I own a restaurant before attempting to purchase anything there as the prices would require that kind of cash flow.

No, I never found a big poacher. I curled him up in my turkey roaster and cooked him just fine, though. But if you too have found that poaching a salmon has lost some of its romantic appeal, these menus with salmon should provide plenty of *oh la la* inspiration.

19

Whole Poached Salmon If You Must
Green Mayonnaise
Salad of Zucchini and Yellow Squash and Tomato
Grand Marnier Rice Pudding

Serves four

Yes, I realize there are definitely times when poaching a salmon is the only conceivable cooking method. The cooked salmon is then good hot or cold, of course, and looks good and makes you look good. If you plan to poach the fish and serve it cold you may want to consider decorating it the way the guys in the tall white hats do. Let the fish cool after poaching it and peel the skin off the body. Gently scrape the thin layer of grey meat off with a knife. Layer halved slices of cucumber in rows over the body so the cucumber resembles large fish scales. Cherry tomatoes are nice for an eye patch and of course good ol' hard-boiled eggs can be used for the bordering. Use your imagination and plan on this taking a while. But, in my opinion, decorating is completely unnecessary if the salmon is going to be served to fishermen; they like the way he looks just fine.

The rice pudding looks most attractive when served in a glass bowl.

WHOLE POACHED SALMON IF YOU MUST

1 whole salmon, gutted and scaled
  Your liquid should be ⅔ water
    and ⅓ wine. For each bottle
    of wine add:
½ cup vinegar
2 quarts water
2 onions, chopped
1 carrot, chopped
3 shallots, chopped
  Salt and pepper
1 bay leaf
1 tsp. thyme
6 parsley stems
3 whole peppercorns

Combine all the ingredients except for the fish. You may use red wine for a nice change. Cook this court bouillon 30 minutes and let cool. Wrap the salmon well in cheese cloth and, if you decide to remove the head, be sure to cover the end with tin foil. Cook the fish on a rack with the court bouillon reaching just to the rack. Simmer at 200° for 8 minutes per pound.

GREEN MAYONNAISE

4 tbsp. vinegar and lemon juice,
    mixed
¾ tsp. salt
1 tsp. prepared mustard
    A few grinds of pepper
    A dash of cayenne pepper
4 egg yolks
    2½ cups good corn or peanut oil
    A big handful of destemmed
      spinach leaves
3 tbsp. shallots, chopped very fine
1 cup watercress leaves
¼ cup parsley leaves
2 tbsp. dried basil reconstituted
    with a few tablespoons of hot
    water
    Any herbs blanched in a small
      amount of water for 30
      seconds and puréed.

Beat salt, mustard, vinegar and lemon juice together. Add egg yolks. Whisk until foamy. Slowly add oil. Add herbs near end. Finish up and season to taste. If adding salt, dissolve in a little hot water first. It may all be made quickly and easily in a food processor.

SALAD OF ZUCCHINI AND YELLOW SQUASH AND TOMATO

1 head Boston lettuce or 2 bibb,
    cleaned
3 tiny yellow squash, julienned
2 tiny zucchini, julienned
1 tomato, skinned, seeded,
    drained and julienned
    Corn oil or cooking oil
2 tbsp. good vinegar
    Salt and pepper
1 tsp. good prepared mustard
⅓ cup olive oil
    Fresh basil leaves—the little-
    leafed kind, if possible, called
    spiley globe

First mix salt and pepper and vinegar and then add the olive oil, mustard, and basil leaves and zip in the blender for a second or two. Sauté zucchini and yellow squash in corn oil until they just begin to cook. Be sure they keep some of their crispness. Let cool. Toss with lettuce, tomatoes and dressing, or you can keep the squashes separate and lay the alternate colors out in groups on top of the lettuce. Taste for salt and pepper.

GRAND MARNIER RICE PUDDING

½ cup rice, cooked in water
½-¾ cup yellow raisins
¾ cup, plus 4 tbsp. Grand Marnier
¾ cup light cream
¾ cup milk
    Peel of 1 orange, grated
1 envelope of gelatin
4 egg yolks
    A pinch of salt
⅓ cup sugar
1 cup heavy cream

Rinse the rice in a strainer under warm water and put in 250° oven to dry a little. Fluff with a fork a few times. In a small pot with ¼ cup water and ¾ cup Grand Marnier add the raisins and bring to simmer. Cook until raisins are plump and liquid almost evaporated. Combine the light cream and milk in a small pot and add the grated orange. Bring to scald. Remove from heat and let sit for 40 minutes to infuse the flavor. Strain orange rind out.

Melt the envelope of gelatin in a custard cup with 2 tablespoons of water. Set in small pan on low heat to melt. Whisk the egg yolks, pinch of salt, and sugar together. Add the milk and cream mixture to it. While whisking cook on medium-high or high heat. Add dissolved gelatin and stir constantly until thick. It will become thick quite suddenly. Strain immediately onto rice and stir. Add raisins. Stir. Add 3 tablespoons Grand Marnier. Taste and add more if you like. Whip the heavy cream and add to it any raisin juice and 1 tablespoon Grand Marnier. Whip only to be very soft—no peaks. Stir the custard/rice mixture with a large rubber spatula, resting over a bowl of ice and water. Be sure to let the custard bowl touch the ice water. Stir constantly but lightly as the gelatin sets. Stir until a path through the center of the mixture remains bare for a second. Then stir in ¼ of the whipped cream. Mix well, then fold in the rest of the whipped cream. Gently turn into an oiled mold and let sit in the refrigerator until set. You can do this the day before. Unmold just before serving. Serve alone or with sliced berries topped with a little sugar.

Salmon Scallops
Watercress Salad
Potato Gratin
Grand Marnier Soufflé

Serves four

Using very good prepared mustards that are not too hot and that tout herbs on their labels is critical to making a good salad dressing. Some cities (Boston and London for certain) have stores where their sole purpose in life is to sell different mustards. Next time your rich brother-in-law goes to London, tell him he can make points by bringing you back some fancy mustard.

SALMON SCALLOPS

8 ¼″ salmon scallops, cut from
    fillets, about 2 lbs. in all
2 tbsp. shallots, chopped very,
    very fine
¼ cup cider vinegar or lemon juice,
    strained
½ cup very dry white wine
2 sticks or 8 oz. unsalted butter at
    room temperature
Salt and pepper

Combine shallots, vinegar, wine, a little salt and a grind of pepper. Simmer *slowly* until reduced by ⅓. This you can do ahead. Sauté the salmon very quickly in a couple of tablespoons or so of butter, to count of 3 or 4 each side. Remove to platter or plates. Spoon fat out of pan. Add the vinegar mixture to the fish pan. Scrape around for goodies and on very low heat whisk in the butter slowly to make a foaming sauce. Taste for seasoning. Add salt and pepper if necessary. Serve over fish.

WATERCRESS SALAD

 1 bunch watercress without stems,
    washed
 2 bibb or 1 head Boston lettuce,
    washed
 ½ head red lettuce, washed
 2 tbsp. wine vinegar
 1 tsp. prepared mustard
    Salt and pepper
 1 tsp. soy sauce
 1 garlic clove, peeled and crushed
 ⅓ cup good quality olive oil

Rub salad bowl with garlic. Combine in the blender the vinegar, mustard, soy sauce and salt and pepper and zip on high for a second or two. Add olive oil and blend again. Toss with the greens and serve with a crusty bread and butter and a couple of cheeses.

POTATO GRATIN

 4-6 Idaho potatoes
 2-plus cups cream
 1 tbsp. unsalted butter—soft
    Salt and pepper
    Nutmeg, whole to grate
 1 clove garlic
 ¼ cup fontina cheese, grated
    (optional)

Rub a medium size baking dish with the peeled garlic clove. Let dry. Then grease with the butter. Peel and slice potatoes very thin. Make a layer of potatoes covering the bottom. Cover with cream. Season with salt and pepper and nutmeg. Add another layer of potatoes, putting in the cheese here if you like, then more cream and salt and pepper, nutmeg, etc. Top with a layer of cream. Bake in a 300° oven for at least an hour or until butter starts to bubble around the edge. Let sit 10 minutes at least before serving.

GRAND MARNIER SOUFFLÉ

  4 tbsp. Grand Marnier
      Grated rind of one small
        orange—optional
  1 cup milk
  3 tbsp. flour
  5 tbsp. sugar, plus some for
        dusting
  4 eggs, separated
  1 extra egg white
      Pinch salt
  2 tbsp. soft butter
  1 vanilla bean
      Confectioners' sugar

Butter and sugar a 6-cup soufflé mold. Stir the flour with a tablespoon or so of the cold milk. Bring to a boil the rest of the milk with 4 heaping tablespoons of sugar and the vanilla bean. Remove from heat and let sit for 10 minutes. Stir in flour mixture (and orange rind if used). Stir over medium high heat until mixture thickens. Stirring continually until it just boils, remove from heat. Continue to stir. Add the egg yolks one by one to sauce. Whisking well after each addition, whisk in the butter and the Grand Marnier. Beat the 5 egg whites and a pinch of salt together until it reaches the soft peak stage. Add 1 tablespoon sugar and beat until stiff and a whole egg in its shell will sit on top of the whites sinking in only ⅓ of the way. Stir ¼ of the whites into the milk, yolk, sugar mixture and then fold in the rest of the whites. Put in mold. It should only be ¾ full. Cook at 375° for about 15-20 minutes. Then, during the last 10 minutes of cooking, open the oven door and quickly sprinkle the top with confectioners' sugar. Do this a few times for a glaze. Soufflé will be done in about ½ hour in all. Be sure it is cooked through. Serve immediately, of course.

Salmon Medallions with Basil-Black Olive Butter
Fiddleheads with Fried Bread Crumbs
Julienned Carrots
Poached Pears and Figs
Sugar Cookies

Serves four

In *Gray's Wild Game Cookbook*, there is quite a long description of the Chet Reneson method of cleaning fiddleheads. The method involves dressing in full sou'wester outfit and tearing down a long lake in a motorboat, holding up each fiddlehead as you speed along, in hopes of getting the chaff off. This description produced several letters from readers, either querying what the heck were fiddleheads or suggesting their own rather bizarre and unprintable techniques for removing the chaff from fiddleheads.

Fiddleheads are baby ferns, very delicious greens. It is possible to get the chaff off by plunging them in boiling water for a few minutes and then draining and rinsing and patting them dry on a towel that you intend to throw away after the fiddleheads are clean. This must be repeated multiple times and is very tedious work. Try to pick the ones that are clean or find them already clean and in cellophane at your grocer.

SALMON MEDALLIONS

4 salmon steaks about ¾" thick
3 tbsp. unsalted butter
Salt and pepper

To prepare the salmon medallions, first slice from a whole, cleaned salmon four ¾" steaks. This can be done with a still-frozen, but gutted, fish by using a saw. This has the advantage of giving you just what you need at the time and returning the rest of the salmon to the freezer for future use. Or, with a fresh fish, use a sharp knife and a cleaver to get through the backbone. Now with a pair of small pliers remove all needle bones from the four steaks. You can feel these by running your fingers over the flesh. Remember to do both sides. With a very sharp knife remove the skin and the center backbone from each salmon steak, now you will have two pieces from each salmon steak. Lay the pieces down as if they were still attached and then flip one upside down so that the fat parts face each other and the thin parts go off in opposite directions. Now wrap the thin parts around in their natural curve (they will both be going in the same direction) and push four toothpicks in to hold together. You should now have a round, boneless salmon steak called a medallion. You can do all this in the morning and then put the medallions on a plate covered with some plastic wrap in the refrigerator until dinner. To cook the salmon, melt the butter in a fry pan over medium-high heat. Put the salmon in and cook this first side for 4-6 minutes, the second side for just a few minutes (remember fish continues to cook even though it's been removed from the heat so remove the salmon when the center of each medallion is still a little bit darker pink). Place each medallion on a warm plate and season with salt and pepper. Put the compound butter immediately on top.

BLACK OLIVE AND BASIL BUTTER

1 stick unsalted butter
2 tbsp. dried basil reconstituted in
    2 tbsp. hot water
4 oil-cured black olives with pits
    removed and chopped finely
Lemon juice
Salt and pepper

Let the butter soften and then whip it till fluffy. Squeeze out the water from the reconstituted basil and add basil to the butter. Combine the butter and basil with the chopped olives. Add salt, pepper and lemon juice to your taste and then whip again. Turn the butter mixture out onto a large piece of plastic wrap and roll it up, shaping it as you roll into a log. Freeze for 24 hours, bringing it out of the refrigerator an hour or so before the salmon is cooked. Use a cookie cutter to cut the butter pats for atop the salmon. (The remainder of the butter can be used in soup or as a nice sandwich spread. Keeps 1 month in the freezer).

FIDDLEHEADS WITH FRIED BREAD CRUMBS

1 lb. fiddleheads, cleaned and
    blanched
3 tbsp. hard bread crumbs
1 cup clarified butter
2 tbsp. unsalted butter
¼ tsp. chopped garlic
    Salt and pepper

For the bread crumbs, heat the clarified butter and add to it the garlic and bread crumbs. Sauté until the bread crumbs are a nice golden brown and then season with salt and pepper. Now sauté the blanched fiddleheads in 2 tablespoons of butter until they are hot. Toss the bread crumbs and fiddleheads together and check for seasoning. Serve immediately.

JULIENNED CARROTS

8-10 nice sized carrots
2 tbsp. unsalted butter
1 tbsp. fresh parsley, chopped fine
    Salt and pepper

Scrape the outside of each carrot with a vegetable peeler and cut into 2-inch lengths. Now julienne into ⅛-inch sticks. Blanch in boiling water for about 5 minutes or until just tender and then drain. Sauté the carrots quickly in butter, adding the parsley, salt and pepper to your taste.

POACHED PEARS AND FIGS

          1 vanilla bean, split
          2 cloves
          2 cups water
        ½ cup sugar
        ¼ lb. dried figs
        ½ lb. dried pears (fresh, still-hard
                 pears can be used, too. In this
                 case, peel and core the pears.)

Bring to a boil the first four ingredients and let simmer 5 to 10 minutes. Add the figs, cover, and cook very gently until they are soft, about 45 minutes. Add the pears and continue to cook for another 15 minutes. Remove the fruit and reduce the syrup over a high heat by ¼. Serve with the syrup and crème fraiche.

SUGAR COOKIES

        ¾ cup unsalted butter, softened
        ½ cup sugar
          1 tsp. grated orange rind
          1 egg
          2 cups cake flour
        ¼ tsp. salt
              Dash of vanilla

Cream the butter into the sugar and salt. Whip till fluffy. Add 1 egg, orange rind and vanilla and mix. Blend in the flour. Refrigerate the dough, covered, until it is firm. Roll out in small batches and cut with a cookie cutter. Sprinkle with cinnamon sugar and bake at 350° till just starting to brown around the edges (about 7 minutes or so).

Fresh Mozzarella Slices
Grilled Whole Salmon
Rice Pilaf
Peas and Artichoke Hearts
Raspberry Tart

Serves four

A good homemade tart pastry is, to my way of thinking, one of the most difficult items to make. Little French girls learn at their mothers' sides and have the advantage of years of practice. Big American girls learn at the side of their cooking instructor and anonymously leave piles of grey dough on the instructor's doorstep in frustration and anger. If you master the technique for good tart pastry you will most certainly be rewarded by the *oohs* and *ahhs* of your guests. I do believe that pastry making is something that cannot be described in a cookbook; you must see someone do it. Consequently, if you haven't had the chance to observe an expert at work, use frozen Pepperidge Farm pastry sheets. They are a whole lot better than grey piles of dough.

FRESH MOZZARELLA SLICES

As a first course, thinly slice fresh mozzarella or otalegio cheese. Drizzle good olive oil on it and sprinkle with cracked black pepper. Serve with homemade bread.

GRILLED WHOLE SALMON

Clean the salmon and remove the head. Also scrape the scales off. Wash the cavity well with fresh water and sprinkle the cavity with salt and pepper and your choice of herbs. Brush the salmon's skin with olive oil or butter. Heat the grill till very hot, a gas grill for 20 minutes. While this is happening, measure the girth of the fish at the thickest point. Calculate the number of inches times ten and that's your approximate total cooking time for both sides of the fish.

RICE PILAF

2 cups rice
½ cup unsalted butter
4 cups hot chicken stock (If using
    cubes to make stock, Knorr is
    preferable.)

Melt the butter in a large pan with a lid. Sauté the rice in the butter until quite hot and add the stock. Lower the heat to a simmer and put a towel over the pan and then the lid. Cook about 25 minutes depending on the depth of the pan. The rice is done when the grains are plump and separate and all the liquid has been absorbed.

PEAS AND ARTICHOKE HEARTS

2 lbs. fresh peas
2 8 oz. cans of artichoke hearts in
    brine
2 oz. pancetta, chopped fine
3 tbsp. unsalted butter
    Salt and pepper

Several hours before, drain the artichoke hearts and rinse in lukewarm water. Let sit in a bowl of cool water, changing the water at least twice and the tinny taste should be gone. Drain and slice into quarters. While you're waiting for the artichokes to bathe, shell the peas. Blanch in boiling salted water for a minute or two, drain and plunge into ice water. Drain again and set aside. In a large saucepan, combine pancetta and butter and fry on medium heat for a few minutes. Add the artichoke hearts and heat thoroughly. Add the peas and cook till hot. Season with salt and fresh cracked pepper.

RASPBERRY TART

        1   recipe your best pastry or
              Pepperidge Farm's
        2   cups heavy cream
       ½   lb. cream cheese (not whipped
              cream cheese)
     1½   tbsp. vanilla
        3   tbsp. confectioners' sugar
1½ to 2   pints raspberries
       ½   cup red currant jelly
        1   tbsp. framboise
            Cheese cloth

Do this the night before. First whip the cream cheese. Then whip the heavy cream together with the sugar and vanilla until it is over-whipped and great clumps fall from the the whisk. Now mix ¼ to ⅓ of the heavy cream into the cream cheese and mix well. Fold in the remaining heavy cream. Rinse the cheese cloth in cold water and line a colander with it. Pour in the cream mixture and place in the refrigerator on a plate for overnight. If whipped and folded well, water should ooze out onto the plate.

Preheat the oven to 425° for at least 20 minutes. Roll out the pastry and line a buttered tart pan with it. Prick with a fork and line the pastry with tin foil and fill with rice, beans or pastry weights. Put in the oven for about 7 minutes. Remove the foil and weights and sprinkle with granulated sugar. Return the shell to the oven for another 5 to 7 minutes or until the pastry begins to caramelize. Remove from the oven and let cool for a minute or two, then remove from the pan onto a cooling rack. This can be done several hours before if you like, and if it isn't too humid out.

To serve, melt the red currant jelly in a small saucepan with framboise. Fill the pastry shell with the cream mixture and cover the top with raspberries, right side up. Paint the berries with jelly and framboise mixture and serve.

Salmon Hash Patties
Sage Bread
Three Green Salad

Serves four

I do believe that the different species of salmon are different from each other in taste. Certainly the Pacific salmon taste different from the Atlantic and the everywhere salmon, the coho, different from them. The meat of the Atlantic salmon is quite a bit paler than other salmon and seems to have a lighter, more delicate flavor. I prefer the Atlantic salmon. Is that because I live on the Atlantic ocean? But for this recipe the best salmon would be the more hearty-flavored coho; or actually the best salmon for this recipe is the the one that has been cooked and in your refrigerator and needs to be used up.

SALMON HASH PATTIES

2 cups leftover cooked salmon, no
    bones or skin, and flaked
1 very small onion, chopped fine
1 small celery stick, chopped fine
1 large Idaho potato, cooked and
    mashed
2 eggs, beaten lightly
¼ cup butter
    Flour for dredging
    Salt and pepper

Sauté the onion and celery in 2 tablespoons of the butter until they are wilted. Place the salmon in a mixing bowl with the cooked onion and celery plus the eggs and potato. Season with salt and pepper and a little chopped parsley if you like. Form into patties and dip lightly in flour. Sauté in the remaining butter until golden.

34

SAGE BREAD

      1   package yeast
    2⅓   cups all-purpose unbleached
             white flour
      ⅔   cup whole wheat flour
      1   tsp. oil
      1   tsp. salt
    1½   tsp. dried sage (not ground)

In a round bowl mix the yeast with 1 cup of the all-purpose flour and enough warm water to form a cohesive ball of dough, but keep it gooey. Mark an × on top and then fill the bowl with warm water. Let sit 5 to 15 minutes and the ball will pop up to the surface. While the sponge rests mix the remaining flours, salt, and sage together. Add the oil and enough room-temperature water to form another ball but this one should be very dry. When the sponge pops up scoop it out of the water and add it to the dry ball. Knead together for 6 minutes or until the dough is firm and elastic. Let rise in a lightly-oiled bowl covered tightly with plastic wrap for about 2 hours or until doubled in bulk. Punch down and then shape into a loaf by flattening it out and rolling it up tightly. Then again flatten it in the other direction and roll it up, pinching loose ends together. This will allow the bread to keep its shape. Place on floured baking sheet and make slashes with a knife on top of the loaf. Let rise till almost doubled in bulk. It should take less time this rising, approximately an hour or so. Preheat oven to 400° for 30 minutes. If you use baking tiles put them in, if not put in another baking sheet to preheat also. Just before baking, re-slash the bread and sprinkle baking sheet with cornmeal. Then carefully roll bread off onto hot baking surface. Bake for 35 to 40 minutes. Let cool on a rack.

THREE GREEN SALAD

At least three different greens; endive, watercress, Boston lettuce or whatever is available to you

6 strips of cooked bacon
½ cup olive oil

3 tbsp. wine vinegar
2 tsp. good prepared mustard
1 tbsp. mayonnaise
¼ tsp. garlic, chopped fine or squeezed through a press
A dash of soy sauce
Salt and pepper

Combine the vinegar, salt and pepper, mustard, garlic and soy sauce. Add the oil and mix well. Now add the mayonnaise and mix well again. Toss dressing with the greens. Crumble the bacon into the salad and toss again.

Leftover Salmon Salad
Tuscan Muffins
Another Grand Marnier Soufflé

Serves four

Why do we have two Grand Marnier soufflé recipes in this book? Recipes have different styles and suit individuals differently. That's why so many cookbooks are sold. The end result for each of these soufflés is the same, a delicious dessert, but you may find one recipe is easier and produces tastier results than the other. Try them both and stick with whatever works for you.

LEFTOVER SALMON SALAD

Cooked salmon, broken into
    chunks
2 small zucchini
2 cucumbers
2 ripe tomatoes
Homemade mayonnaise
Fresh basil, preferably small leaf
Salt and pepper
1 tsp. grated lemon rind
2 tbsp. corn oil
Lettuce

Peel and seed the cucumber. Slice into ⅛" pieces; salt and let drain. Peel, seed, drain and coarsely chop the tomatoes. Cut the zucchini in half the long way and then slice into ⅛" pieces. Sauté in a little corn oil.

Combine salmon, mayonnaise, lemon rind, and vegetables. Toss lightly, but well and season to taste. At the last minute, add basil and tomatoes. Toss carefully again. Taste for seasoning and serve on lettuce.

TUSCAN MUFFINS

2¾ cups all-purpose flour
¼ cup whole-wheat flour
1 package dry yeast
1 tsp. salt

In a medium-sized bowl mix one cup of the all-purpose flour with the yeast and add enough warm water (not hot water) to make a moist and cohesive ball. Fill the bowl with enough warm water so the ball is covered. Let sit 5 to 15 minutes until the ball pops to the surface. Meanwhile take the remaining flours and pile on top of the counter. Make a trench in the middle of the pile and add the salt. You will need to add water, a few tablespoons at a time, fluffing it into the flour with your fingers. The mixture should be slightly cohesive but not wet as the yeast/flour ball will be quite wet. When the ball has risen to the surface of the water, scoop it out and gather the two doughs together into one cohesive ball, kneading as little as possible. When they are altogether and well blended, roll the ball into a cylinder about 2″ in diameter. With a sharp knife cut off muffins about ½″ to ¾″ thick. Dust both sides with flour and set on a baking sheet. Each muffin should be several inches from the next. Cook in a preheated oven of 400° till they are golden brown and hollow sounding to the tap (about 20 minutes). Let cool on racks and serve with unsalted butter. They are quite dense, but marvelous tasting.

ANOTHER GRAND MARNIER SOUFFLÉ

4 egg yolks
5 egg whites and a pinch of salt
4 tbsp. sugar and some for dusting
3 tbsp. flour
8 tbsp. milk

4½ tbsp. Grand Marnier liqueur
1 tbsp. vanilla extract
1 tsp. grated orange rind
Butter to grease the soufflé dish

In heavy saucepan mix sugar, flour, orange rind and milk slowly together. Bring slowly to a boil and stir till mixture thickens. Remove from heat and cool slightly. Then add yolks one by one, beating after each addition. Add vanilla extract and liqueur. In separate large bowl, beat salt and egg whites until they hold a whole uncooked egg, letting the egg sink in only ¼ to ⅓ of the way. Stir ⅓ of the egg white mixture into the base mixing well. Then fold in the remaining whites. Have ready a buttered and sugared 6-cup soufflé mold. Fill with the soufflé, tap on counter once to release any large air pockets and cook in a 400° preheated oven for 30-35 minutes.

Smoked Salmon Salad
Fried Broccoli
Fresh French Whole-wheat Bread
Fruit and Cheeses

Serves four

Fresh homemade bread is the best. In France you learn to truly appreciate how fresh bread (that means only a few hours old) enhances the meal. The bakeries there bake bread twice a day and you buy your bread twice a day. I've read that an average French person will eat a pound of bread a day. I find this completely understandable having lived with their bread for a while. Although it is not in our tradition to go out twice a day for bread, it is possible to find very fresh bread at local gourmet shops or bakeries. This is worth the trip for this meal.

SMOKED SALMON SALAD

4 portions of smoked salmon
   (about 2 cups)
1 red onion, peeled and sliced thin
2-3 tbsp. Armagnac
1 orange
   Olive oil
   Salt and fresh ground pepper

Cut both ends off the orange. Stand the orange on one of the squared off ends and with a large, very sharp knife, cut away both the peel and the pith (the white part) from the top to bottom. When finished, you will have a completely peeled orange. Now separate and remove the sections (a small knife is best to cut between the sections.) Place orange pieces on a plate and set aside.

Place the peeled sliced onion in a small saucepan with a lid. Add a bit of olive oil. Steam over low heat till partially cooked (to remove the onion taste) but still a wee bit crunchy. Raise the lid and toss in the Armagnac. Replace the lid and remove from the heat to steep for a few minutes. Divide the onion between four plates using your judgment as to quantity. You may not need it all. Season with salt and pepper. Top with the smoked salmon. Dribble with good green olive oil and place the orange segments around the edges.

FRIED BROCCOLI

1 head broccoli, separated into
    florets with 1-1½" stems
½ cup flour
    Salt and pepper
    Grated lemon rind from 1 lemon
1 beaten egg
    Milk to moisten to the right
      texture
    Olive oil for frying

Blanch the broccoli in boiling water until it is almost tender, but not quite. Refresh the broccoli in ice water, drain and let dry. Now combine the flour, salt and pepper, lemon rind, egg and enough milk so the mixture is a good-consistency batter. Dip the broccoli in the batter. Fry in hot olive oil. Drain on paper towels and serve at once with a lemon wedge if desired.

Salmon Calzone
Green Salad
Brownies

Serves four

    Cintra has the nice tradition of giving brownies as a birthday present. This is a particularly nice gift when your birthday is in the summer and the children are away at camp. It also is a particularly nice gift because they are particularly nice brownies.

    Calzone is a loaf of bread with stuff in the middle (usually meat or fish). It is very good for Sunday suppers or mother-in-law lunches or cold in a picnic driving to your favorite grouse covert.

SALMON CALZONE

2⅔ cups all-purpose flour
⅓ cup whole wheat flour
1 pkg. dry yeast
3 tsp. dried tarragon, revived
1 tsp. salt
1½ cups cooked salmon, broken into
    pieces
⅔ cup cooked rice
⅓ cup white wine, seasoned with
    salt and pepper
1 small onion, chopped fine and
    sautéed in 2 tbsp. butter
Salt and pepper
1 tbsp. chopped parsley

In a medium–sized mixing bowl mix 1 cup of the flour with the yeast and add enough warm water (not hot water) to make a moist and cohesive ball. Fill the bowl with warm water so the ball is covered. Let sit 5 to 15 minutes until the ball pops to the surface. Meanwhile take the remaining amount of flour and put it on top of the counter. Make a trench in the middle and add salt. Revive the tarragon by mixing it with a little hot water. Put 2 tablespoons of the revived tarragon in the trench (save the third tablespoon for later). You will need to add more water, fluffing it into the flour with your fingers. The mixture should be slightly cohesive but not wet, as the yeast/flour ball will be quite wet. When the ball has risen to the surface of the water, scoop it out and set it in the middle of your flour pile. Knead the flour and the ball together and continue to knead for 5 to 8 minutes or so. Put the dough in an oiled or floured bowl with a towel over it and place in a warm spot to let rise two hours or until doubled in bulk. Punch down and roll out into a 3″×12″ rectangle. Sauté the chopped onion and mix all together with the salmon, cooked rice, wine, parsley and the remaining revived tarragon and taste for seasoning. Lay on bread and close bread up, tightly pinching seam. Flip so seam is on the bottom. Let rise about 1 hour and bake in a 425° preheated oven (on tiles if you have them, on the bottom oven shelf) for about 35-40 minutes. Let cool to room temperature before serving.

THE BEST BROWNIES

2 squares unsweetened chocolate
1 stick unsalted butter
1 cup sugar
2 eggs
1 tsp. vanilla
¼ cup flour
¼ tsp. salt
1 cup chopped walnuts

Preheat oven to 325°. Melt together the chocolate and butter and then stir in the sugar. Beat together the eggs and vanilla and add them to the chocolate mixture. Now quickly stir in the flour, salt and chopped nuts. Spread in greased 8″×8″ pan and bake 40-45 minutes at 325°. Do not overcook or they will be dry. Cake tester should just come out clean. Let cool in pan. Then cut in squares and remove. The first brownie will be hard to get out and may stick and crumble. Do not be deterred. These are the best brownies.

Saltwater Fish

O ne of the great advantages of being a fisherman is that you can only come home with the local, and consequently freshest, fish (as opposed to being enticed into trying fresh mako shark when you are at a fish store in Chicago). No matter how adamant the Dallas waiter is that his ten-pound lobster flown in from Nova Scotia is the best in the world, I know that the one-pound lobster I get from my friend who scuba dives for them off this Massachusetts beach is the best. It's not just because it's the freshest, but because now, as a twenty-year resident of New England, I have learned that the biggest lobsters are not necessarily the tastiest, just as I know that the snapper blues (bluefish in the 1- to 2-pound range) are great grilled whole and the regular blues should be steaked.

There is no better guide to the cook than local lore. Ed and I were fortunate to be able to travel to France with our children for a two week stay with some friends in a chateau. The meals were cooked by madame (the caretaker's wife) but we did the obtaining of the food. We purchased from the local market the only fish large enough to feed us all, a *merlu*. It was a rather ugly looking bottom feeding type of fish which turned out to be similar to our hake. Certainly a respectable fish but not one I would have spent much time on. Madame made a lovely court bouillion and then a simple *beurre-blanc* to go over it, a recipe I would have reserved for salmon. It was wonderful; she knew how to cook her own local fish.

I will not profess to know more than you do about a fish that surrrounds you. You will note that I have not included in this book every type of fish that you can sportfish for and eat. I do not know that much and will not include a fish I know absolutely nothing about just for the sake of inclusion. With a fish that is not one of my most familiar fish I have tried at least to use some imagination with it—after all, redfish doesn't always have to be blackened.

There is one word of caution that must be thrown into this local lore concept. I spent nearly six months working at a hospital in northern Newfoundland. We lived in the orphanage which was next door to the hospital and down the street from the fish docks and local fish cannery. We ate cod three meals a day for six months. It was very fresh and it was certainly being cooked by the locals and it was really terrible. I have come to believe that the cod was bad partially because we ate it so much, and partially because the cook had no concept of when the fish had finished cooking. Her adage seemed to be, when in doubt cook for five hours, and she was always in doubt. Certainly "doneness" in fish cannot be reduced to precise minutes of time, as with a cake. There are too many variables to each fish for that. His size, the thickness of the fillet or steak, the amount of water left in the fish and how cold it is all change cooking time. It is definitely better to learn to rely on seeing, tasting, smelling, and touching a fish for doneness. Always, always a fish should be cut into and tasted before serving. The first bluefish I ever had was served by a hostess whose gas stove had run out of propane but she'd decided to serve it anyway. I nearly never ate bluefish again. Undone fish is really revolting, but taste the fish before you think it's done. It can always be cooked more, but over-cooking is impossible to undo. The cooking times in this book are always to be regarded as approximates, and you will notice that in some cases I have not written a time. This is because your seeing and smelling and tasting the fish are better guides to its doneness than something cast into the words of a book. Don't trust books on this stuff, trust yourself.

Inshore Saltwater Fish

One time I went fishing with David on his 25-foot cabin cruiser. It had been one of those last-minute, it's-such-a-beautiful-day, let's-go-fishing, trips. Ed was working too hard and couldn't go, but I had only to drag along one baby—and find the right fishing equipment in the garage. I was pretty used to saltwater fishing but rarely (if ever) went fishing without Ed. And Ed was king of equipment in our household. He wasn't what you would call manic about the care of the hunting and fishing equipment. In fact he was what you really would call casual. Rust and saltwater corrosion were on intimate terms with all our equipment. But he did have the distinct advantage of knowing where in that great expansive morass of stuff even the tiniest fly would be hiding. I did not have this advantage, if the stuff in front of me looked like it could catch a fish, grab it. What did it matter if we were going mackerel fishing and I had grabbed a surfcasting rod, or if the lighter weight rod had white stuff all over the ferrules—they were both fishing rods, weren't they?

The little rod had been real hard to put together, but I'd fixed it up with a jigging rig, David had purchased some Cokes and bait all at the same stop, and the baby was cooing in his little seat on the deck of the boat. We were ready to go. We steamed out of the Gloucester harbor. We spent an hour or two bobbing along, dipping the rods rhythmically, playing with the baby, watching him be lulled to sleep by the rocking of the boat. We talked, and ate, and drank beer and let the sun beat on us. We would anchor and fish, then move and troll. David got a bluefish right off, then we waited a long time. Then, *wham*, David's jigging rig tugged and wiggled and bent and looked 25 pounds heavier; then, *wham*, mine did too! Scrambling for the rods before they'd flip out of the holders, we began to crank and pull and crank and pull. As the lines shortened we both realized we each had four fish on at once. We were both yelling gleefully back and forth about our prosperity, trying to drive the boat, and get the fish all inside the boat. The baby had tipped over strapped in his chair and lay crying on his stomach with arms and legs flailing, the chair on his back turtle-style. This was worse than a Chinese fire drill! With my right hand holding the rod and the left trying to right the baby's seat, David's fish flopped about on the deck. Suddenly the end of my rod fell off and was shooting down the monofilament. I quickly decided to drop the baby and go for the rod tip. Leaning over the side of the boat to grab the other end of the rod, the boat lurched and there was a moment when I thought I would be joining the fish in the water— instead the butt-end of the rod did. Now I was laughing so hard that I was totally useless in trying to retrieve the rod or land the fish. David came to the rescue, boat-hooked the rod, jammed it back together, and brought the mackerel into the boat. I comforted the baby.

Well-maintained equipment is essential both in fishing and in cooking. A rod that falls apart when it's catching a fish and a knife that is too dull to fillet a fish provide the same sad results, nothing to eat. Both cooking and fishing have a tendency to produce equipment maniacs; this is to be avoided. There is as little reason to fill your kitchen with the superfluous pastry crimpers as it is to fill your tackle box with scent for plastic worms. Just give me my well-oiled green Penn reel and a barbeque grill and we'll call it dinner.

Grilled Bluefish
Grilled Polenta
Chicory and Escarole Salad
Melon Ice

Serves four

Polenta is a wonderful item for getting starch into a menu and diet. A form of polenta, not using the cornmeal but a different grain, was carried by the Roman soldiers when they went to fight against Hannibal. A recipe that has stood the test of that kind of time has got to have merit.

GRILLED BLUEFISH

1½-2 lbs. fillets, skin on and
      slashed
1½ sticks unsalted butter
3 medium cloves garlic, chopped
      finely
2 tsp. finely chopped fresh sage
Salt and pepper

Make the compound butter in advance. Whip the butter until light and fluffy. Add salt and pepper, garlic and sage. Mix well and mound onto plastic wrap. Form into a cylinder and freeze for 24 hours. Bring to room temperature before using. Grill fish, flesh side first, 8 minutes per side. When done spread the butter over each fillet and serve.

GRILLED POLENTA

1 cup cornmeal
½ cup unsalted butter
1 cup water
3 cups milk
½ tsp. fresh grated nutmeg
1 onion
   Salt and pepper
   A few slices pancetta, diced

Sauté pancetta until just crispy. Save the fat. Chop onion very fine and sauté in the butter until translucent. Add the milk. Bring it to a boil. Combine water and cornmeal. Stir with a fork, then add to the boiling milk. Lower heat to medium and stir continuously until the mixture is so thick that the wooden spoon stands up in it. Remove from the heat and add the pancetta, nutmeg and salt and pepper to taste. Lightly grease a cookie sheet and spread the polenta into a ½″ thick rectangle. Let stand until cool and hardened, several hours. Cut into squares and paint with melted butter and grill until hot and semi-toasted.

CHICORY AND ESCAROLE SALAD

1 small head escarole, washed and
   dried
1 small head chicory, washed and
   dried
1 head Boston lettuce, washed and
   dried
1 orange in sections and cleaned of
   membranes
1 small shallot and 1 very small
   garlic clove, chopped extra
   fine
1 tbsp. vinegar
   Salt and pepper
   Grated rind of 1 orange
⅓ cup light olive oil
1 tbsp. heavy cream

Combine vinegar, salt and pepper, shallot and garlic. Let stand a bit to dissolve salt, then add oil, cream and orange rind. Mix well. Toss with lettuces and orange segments.

MELON ICE

3 small ripe cantaloupes. You want
about 3 to 4 lbs. flesh
3 tbsp. (approximately) Midori
liqueur or melon flavored
liqueur
6-8 tbsp. confectioners' sugar
Juice from 2 lemons
A pinch of salt

Discard the melon seeds, remove the flesh and purée in a food processor. Then add the remaining ingredients to the purée tasting it as you go for proper flavor. Stir well, chill, taste again for flavor and balance. Make according to your ice cream machine's directions. If the cantaloupe shells are the right size, chill them and use as individual serving containers. Pack the melon sorbet in 4 of the shells and chill thoroughly. Garnish with mint sprigs or cut a strawberry and fan it out.

Bluefish Broiled with Thyme and Noisette Butter
Asparagus
Perfect Tomatoes with Cognac Dressing
Raspberry Ice and Sugar Cookies

Serves four

Cooking bluefish fast and hot, as grilling or broiling does, is preferable, I believe, over baking or poaching or any other method because bluefish is quite an oily fish and needs the high heat to draw out the oil. For the same reason, bluefish is one of those fish that should never be frozen if it can be avoided.

BLUEFISH BROILED WITH THYME AND NOISETTE BUTTER

2 small size bluefish fillets
1 stick unsalted butter
1 tbsp. thyme (preferably fresh)
   Salt and pepper

Heat one stick of butter till foaming and then stir gently with your small size whisk over a high heat until the butter begins to turn a light brown. Remove it from the heat and continue whisking. If it begins to turn a darker brown turn into a cool pot and whisk. If it gets black, throw it out and start again. Paint the bluefish fillets with the butter and sprinkle with thyme. Broil the fish until done and then season with salt and pepper. Pour any remaining butter over the fish and serve with lemon wedges.

ASPARAGUS

3 lbs. asparagus (or 6 to 10 spears
      per person, depending on the
      fatness of the spears)
   Melted butter
   Salt and pepper

Cut or break off the bottom end of each asparagus stalk and peel with a vegetable peeler. Peeling asparagus makes them taste better, look less nasty and will impress your mother, so it's worth it.
    Steam over boiling water until just tender when pierced with a fork. The asparagus should resist the fork just a little. Serve immediately with melted butter and salt and pepper.

PERFECT TOMATOES WITH COGNAC DRESSING

6 or 8 tomatoes
½ cup light olive oil
1 tbsp. red wine vinegar
1 tbsp. cognac
1 tsp. mustard
¼ cup heavy cream
Salt and pepper

Mix the vinegar, cognac, mustard and dashes of salt and pepper. Whisk the cognac mixture together with the olive oil and the cream. Let sit for at least one hour. Immerse each tomato in boiling water for 10 seconds and put immediately into a cold water bath. Peel and slice the tomatoes and arrange attractively on a platter. Lightly sprinkle with salt and pepper and then dribble the dressing over the tomatoes.

RASPBERRY ICE WITH SUGAR COOKIES

8 cups raspberries
1 cup sugar
1 tbsp. framboise (raspberry
    liqueur)
Pinch of salt

Clean berries and purée in the blender. You should have one quart of purée. Boil the sugar in ½ cup water for five minutes, then let cool. Add the sugar syrup a little at a time to the purée, stirring all the time and occasionally checking the taste for sweetness. You may not need all of the sugar syrup; sweeten it to your taste. Add the salt and framboise and chill. Freeze according to your ice cream machine's directions.

For a good sugar cookie recipe, see page 30.

Broiled Striped Bass with Wild Mushrooms and Tomato
Peas and Artichoke Hearts
Chocolate Roll

Serves four

It sure is a good thing that grocery stores and gourmet shops are carrying a wider selection of mushrooms, both fresh and dried, because I was coming dangerously close to trying to learn to pick my own wild mushrooms. I probably would have ended up dead. Wild mushrooms are a very tricky business and the best way to learn how to gather the safe ones is to go out in the woods with someone who has identified, picked and eaten wild mushrooms and is still around to be your guide. Stick to one or two species, like puff balls or morels, which are easy to identify, and don't bother with trying to learn a whole broad range of wild mushrooms. And don't rely solely on books to teach you what each mushroom is. Wild mushrooms are spectacularly good, but good from a store, too.

BROILED STRIPED BASS WITH WILD MUSHROOMS AND TOMATO

4 striped bass steaks, about ½
    pound each
4 large tomato slices, seeded and
    drained
1 lb. wild mushrooms—
    chanterelles, morels, etc.
4 tbsp. unsalted butter
  Olive basting oil (See index or
    "Basics" chapter.)
  Salt and pepper
1 tsp. fresh thyme leaves
1 tsp. chopped parsley

Clean (don't wash if possible) and chop mushrooms. Sauté in hot butter until just coated. Lower heat. Season with salt and pepper and add thyme. Cover pan and cook for 5 to 8 minutes until juices start to exude. Remove cover and raise heat and sauté, stirring until golden brown. Season to taste and sprinkle with parsley and set aside. Baste steaks lavishly with the olive basting oil and broil 6 to 8 minutes each side. Place a tomato slice on top of each steak and brush with olive basting oil and broil again until the tomatoes begin to brown, 2 or 3 minutes more. Season with salt and pepper. Top with wild mushrooms and serve at once.

PEAS AND ARTICHOKE HEARTS

2 lbs. fresh peas
2 8-oz. cans of artichoke hearts in
    brine
2 oz. pancetta, chopped fine
3 tbsp. unsalted butter
  Salt and pepper

Several hours before, drain the artichoke hearts and rinse in lukewarm water. Let sit in a bowl of cool water, changing the water at least twice and the tinny taste should be gone. Drain and slice into quarters. While you're waiting for the artichokes to bathe, shell the peas. Blanch in boiling salted water for a minute or two, drain and plunge into ice water. Drain again and set aside. In a large saucepan, combine pancetta and butter and fry on medium heat for a few minutes. Add the artichoke hearts and heat thoroughly. Add the peas and cook till hot. Season with salt and fresh cracked pepper.

CHOCOLATE ROLL

       6 large eggs, separated
       ¾ cup sugar
       6 oz. semi-sweet chocolate
       3 tbsp. strong espresso
          Dusting of dry cocoa
          Pinch of salt
     1½ cups heavy cream
       2 tbsp. liqueur of your choice
       1 tbsp. confectioners' sugar

   Melt chocolate with coffee in double boiler and cool slightly. Beat yolks together and add sugar and continue beating until thick and light. Add chocolate to egg yolk, sugar mixture. Beat whites with a pinch of salt until stiff but not dry. Stir ⅓ of the whites into the yolk, chocolate mixture.
   Gently fold the remaining whites into the chocolate mixture with a large spatula. Carefully spread mixture into a 10"×15" jelly roll pan, greased, lined with wax paper and greased again. Bake 15 minutes in a preheated 350° oven. When done, set pan on rack and cover with a damp kitchen towel. Allow to cool 1 hour and spray with mister one or two times if necessary to keep the cake moist. Sift some cocoa onto a piece of wax paper just a little larger than the jelly roll pan. Turn pan upside down onto cocoa-covered paper and carefully remove cooking wax paper. Beat heavy cream with confectioners' sugar and liqueur until thick. Spread over cake and roll cake up like a jelly roll, leaving seam side down on serving platter. Chill several hours.
   NOTE: Framboise would be a nice liqueur to use if you could add a few handfuls of raspberries to the whipped cream before spreading. Grand Marnier, Amaretto, etc., even rum is nice.

Striped Bass with Lime Mayonnaise
Snow Peas with Peas
Boiled New Potatoes

Serves four

STRIPED BASS WITH LIME MAYONNAISE

1 very small striped bass (about 5
    lbs.) cleaned, gills removed
    and head left on or removed
2 large onions, minced
6 cloves garlic, minced
3 tbsp. unsalted butter

Preheat the oven to 375°. Stuff the cavity of the fish with a few thyme sprigs and season with salt and pepper and place in a large baking dish. Sauté onions and garlic in butter until onions are translucent but not brown. Pour over fish and bake 50 minutes. Flesh will flake when done. Drain off juices and save. If more than 2 tablespoons, cook these juices until reduced to 2 tablespoons and then strain and reserve.

LIME MAYONNAISE

Grated rind of 3 limes
3 egg yolks
½ lb. unsalted butter, melted
3 tbsp. water
1 tbsp. lime juice
½ tsp. salt
3 grinds pepper from a mill

Combine water, lime juice, salt and pepper. Cook over medium heat until reduced to about 1½ tablespoons. Reduce heat to low. Add yolks and whisk until mixture is thick and white. Take off the heat and add the warm butter bit by bit. From time to time dribble in the juices from the cooked fish to prevent the sauce from becoming too thick. Just before serving, add the grated lime rind.

SNOW PEAS WITH PEAS

2 lbs. fresh unshelled peas, blanched, refreshed in ice water and drained, or 1 box frozen peas
1 lb. snow peas, stems and strings from each edge removed and cut in half at an angle, then blanched, refreshed in ice water and drained
1½ tbsp. unsalted butter
Salt and pepper

Heat butter to sizzling and add peas and snow peas. Cook just to heat. Season with salt and pepper.

BOILED NEW POTATOES

Allow 3 small potatoes per person. Sprinkle with chopped parsley and season with salt and pepper.

Broiled Weakfish with Mint and Garlic
Couscous with Wild Mushrooms and Chives
Your Nice Green Salad
Orange Jelly

Serves four

It was not until I was a grown-up that I discovered that in Australia (and probably in several of those other English-speaking countries) they call Jello, "jelly." I can't quite recall what they call our jelly, perhaps just jam. Anyway, it makes it handy that we can use proper English terms for this dessert, because who would want to say they were serving Jello for dessert?

BROILED WEAKFISH WITH MINT AND GARLIC

2 lbs. weakfish fillets
1½ sticks unsalted butter at room
temperature
1 tbsp. plus 1 tsp. dried mint
1 tsp. finely chopped garlic
Salt and pepper
Lemon slices

Reconstitute the mint in warm water. Whip the butter until light and fluffy. Add salt and pepper, garlic and mint. Mix well and mound onto plastic wrap. Form into a cylinder and freeze for 24 hours. Bring to room temperature before using.

Broil the fish about 5 to 8 minutes. Just before done put several pats of the butter on the fish. Return to broiler to finish. Serve with round slices of lemon, the centers removed and filled with mint sprigs.

COUSCOUS WITH WILD MUSHROOMS AND CHIVES

 1 cup couscous
 1 cup chicken broth—Knorr cubes
   are fine
 8 oz. wild mushrooms, depending
   on what your store carries.
   Morels, chanterelles, porcini,
   all are fine.
10 tbsp. unsalted butter
   Salt and pepper
 2 tsp. fresh chives, snipped

Try not to wash the mushrooms unless absolutely necessary. Wipe dry and cut into bite size pieces. If mushrooms are tiny, leave whole. Sauté the mushrooms in 4 tablespoons butter until hot and well coated. Season with salt and pepper, cover pan and lower heat. Cook in this manner for 5 to 6 minutes, then remove cover, raise heat and evaporate liquid. Stir occasionally until mushrooms become golden brown. Remove from heat and let stand. In saucepan, bring chicken stock to a boil with 4 tablespoons butter and salt and pepper. Stir in couscous, cover pan and remove from heat. Let stand about 7 minutes. Mix in mushrooms, 2-3 tablespoons butter and fluff and mix couscous and mushrooms. Add chives. Season to taste and serve.

Serve with a gentle green salad. No harsh greens, no garlic, no onions.

ORANGE JELLY

1½ packages Knox gelatin
 ½ cup cold water
3½ cups boiling water
 ¾ cup white sugar
 3 tbsp. fresh lemon juice
 1 small can frozen orange juice
 1 cup heavy cream
 1 tbsp. confectioners' sugar
 2 tsp. vanilla

Dissolve gelatin in cold water. Add boiling water. Stir thoroughly until gelatin dissolves. Add sugar. Stir again. Add orange juice and lemon juice. Mix well and pour into glass container and chill well. This dessert is somewhat soft compared to "Jello." Whip the heavy cream with the confectioners' sugar and vanilla. Whip so that it is loose and could still be poured. Serve with the "jelly."

Redfish
Potato Flan
Salad of Bibb Lettuce and Bittergreens
Chocolate Cake

Serves four

This redfish is another version of that popular Louisiana recipe. It can be made in a skillet but because of the high heat necessary and the quantities of butter, you will probably have half the country's fire departments in your kitchen before you finish. So do it on a gas grill; charcoal is not hot enough. Preheat gas grill hot, hot, hot. For the salad simply wash and spin dry the two lettuces and use the basic vinaigrette listed in the "Basics" chapter on page 210. This is no ordinary chocolate cake, so chocoholics take note.

REDFISH

4 fish fillets, ½″ thick, sliced in
    half horizontally if they are too
    thick
2 sticks melted unsalted butter
1 tbsp. paprika
¼ tsp. each thyme and oregano
½ tsp. cayenne pepper
½ tsp. each white and black
    pepper, fresh ground
1 tsp. garlic powder
2 tsp. salt

Just before grilling, drown the fillets in the melted butter. Cover the fillets with the last six ingredients and cook 2 minutes each side. When you turn the fish, cover the cooked side with more butter and even more when it is done. This ought to make everyone sit up straight.

POTATO FLAN

1 medium-sized flan, an
    earthenware baking dish
2 lbs. potatoes, peeled and cut
    very thin (use Idaho potatoes)
1½ cups onion, sliced thin and
    sautéed in olive oil until just
    golden
6 tbsp. unsalted butter (soft)
1 crushed garlic clove

3 tbsp. chopped parsley (Italian
    parsley if possible)
Grated rind of 1 lemon
¼ cup chicken broth
½ cup heavy cream
Juice of 1 lemon
Salt and pepper, fresh ground, of
    course

Preheat oven to 375°. Rub the flan with the garlic clove. Let the flan dry and cover the bottom and sides with the butter. Make an even layer of potato slices on the bottom. Season with salt and pepper. Now add a parsley, lemon rind and onion layer, evenly distribute and season with salt and pepper. Keep going and end with potatoes. Mix broth, cream and lemon juice. Season with salt and pepper and pour over. Bake at 375° for 1¾ hours. Serve hot or lukewarm.

CHOCOLATE CAKE

½ lb. (2 sticks) unsalted butter
½ lb. unsweetened chocolate; the
    better the chocolate the better
    the cake
1½ cups sugar
10 eggs, separated
1 tbsp. lemon juice
2 tbsp. orange liqueur (Cointreau)
1 tbsp. vanilla
Pinch of salt
Sprinkle of confectioners' sugar

Combine the butter and chocolate in a saucepan and melt them over a low flame. Add the vanilla, lemon juice, salt and liqueur. Remove from the heat. Beat together the egg yolks and sugar until they ribbon lightly and then combine with the chocolate mixture. Beat the egg whites until they support a whole raw egg without sinking and then stir ⅓ of the whites into the chocolate mixture. Fold in the remaining whites. Butter and flour a 10-inch spring form pan. Cut a 10-inch round of wax paper and butter and flour that, placing it on the bottom of the springform pan. Pour the cake batter into the pan and bake in a preheated oven of 250° for 2½ hours. Let cool completely and remove it from the pan. Sprinkle with confectioners' sugar.

Grilled Lemon-Thyme Mackerel
Tomato and Eggplant Tart
Nice Green Salad

Serves four

Your green salad or ours; see the index or "Basics" chapter for ours.

GRILLED LEMON-THYME MACKEREL

    4 little mackerel
    1 stick softened, unsalted butter
       Salt and pepper
       Grated rind of 1 lemon
    2 tsp. fresh thyme
       Dash of Tabasco

Make the lemon-thyme butter ahead. Whip the butter until fluffy and then add the salt and pepper and lemon rind, thyme and dash of Tabasco. Place in plastic wrap and mold into a log shape. Freeze until an hour before it's to be used, then remove to the refrigerator.

Butterfly fresh mackerel and remove head and tail. Do not baste, but put some sprigs of herbs such as thyme on the coals just before cooking.

Cook flesh side first and serve with several pats of lemon-thyme butter on each fish.

TOMATO AND EGGPLANT TART

1 recipe pastry (semi-puff)
¾ cup ricotta cheese
2 tbsp. finely chopped scallions—a
    little green included
Salt and pepper
3 cups (approximately) baby
    eggplant, cut into ⅛-inch
    slices

1½ lbs. (about 10) plum tomatoes,
    cut into ⅛-inch slices—let
    drain while preparing the tart
¼ cup olive oil basting oil (see
    below)
2 tbsp. fresh basil cut in slices or
    1½ tsp. dried and revived
1½ tbsp. fresh oregano or ½ tsp.
    dried and revived

Olive Oil Basting Oil:

1 c. good olive oil
8 peeled garlic cloves
1½ tsp. thyme
1 bay leaf

Heat on low the above four ingredients for 20-30 minutes. Remove garlic and keep for whatever.

To revive herbs, place in a small quantity of hot water. Stir and let sit for a few minutes and then use.

This tart may be done in individual tart dishes or one large round one or just laid out on a cookie sheet which can look very impressive indeed. Roll out pastry and butter dish. If on a cookie sheet, butter first. Lay pastry on the cookie sheet and turn edges over to form a little rim. Let rest in refrigerator covered for 1 hour.

Slice eggplant and toss with several teaspoons salt and let sit in a colander for 1 hour to drain. Rinse in cold water and dry.

Mix ricotta with scallions and salt and pepper to taste.

Remove pastry from refrigerator and prick with fork all over except edges. Spread with cheese mixture and lay out tomato and eggplant in overlapping slices. Make circles if in a dish or rows on a cookie sheet. Brush with garlic oil and sprinkle with herbs and salt and pepper.

Bake in a preheated 425° oven for 15 minutes on the bottom rack. Lower heat to 375°. Move tart to top rack and cook 10 more minutes or until top is browned. As soon as possible, but with all dexterity, remove tart from cooking container to cooling rack.

Serve hot, warm, or room temperature.

Pasta with Spinach and Artichoke Hearts
Grilled Mackerel
Tuscan Muffins II
Raspberries with Crème Anglais

Serves four

Crème Anglais can be refrigerated after you've made it and saved for instant great desserts as a hard sauce over any fruit.

PASTA WITH SPINACH AND ARTICHOKE HEARTS

6 oz. imported pasta in shapes
such as bows
1 can artichoke hearts in brine
½ lb. fresh spinach
Salt and pepper
1 cup cream
Unsalted butter

Drain canned artichoke hearts and soak in lukewarm water for 20 minutes. Drain. Rinse and soak again. Drain and cut into quarters. Wash the spinach, remove the larger stems and steam until just wilted. Drain well, press water out with a slotted spoon. Chop spinach medium fine and set aside. Reduce cream over medium high heat to ½ cup. Season with salt and pepper. Add spinach and stir well. Add artichokes, stir and taste seasoning. Cook pasta *al dente*. Season with a few pats unsalted butter and salt and pepper. Add sauce. Stir well. Serve with grated Parmesan cheese on the side if you wish it to be more than just a vegetable course.

GRILLED MACKEREL

    4 pounds mackerel, split and
           boned
    ½ stick unsalted butter at room
           temperature
    6 anchovy fillets, chopped coarsely
       Pepper
       A squeeze of lemon juice
    2 tbsp. finely chopped parsley

Whip the butter until light and fluffy. Add anchovies, pepper, lemon juice and parsley. Mix well and mound onto plastic wrap. Form into a cylinder and freeze for 24 hours. Bring to room temperature before using.

Brush the mackerel with olive basting oil (see p. 65) and grill, flesh side first. Just before removing from the grill, put several pats of anchovy butter on each fish.

TUSCAN MUFFINS II

    2¾ cups all-purpose flour
     ¼ cup whole-wheat flour
      1 package dry yeast
      1 tsp. salt
         Several tbsp. of melted pancetta
             fat or bacon fat

In a medium-sized bowl, mix one cup of the all-purpose flour with the yeast and add enough warm water (not hot water) to make a moist and cohesive ball. Fill the bowl with enough warm water so the ball is covered. Let sit 5 to 15 minutes until the ball pops to the surface. Meanwhile take the remaining flours and put on top of the counter. Make a trench in the middle of the pile and add the salt. You will need to add water, a few tablespoons at a time, to the pile, fluffing it into the flour with your fingers. The mixture should be slightly cohesive but not wet, as the yeast/flour ball will be quite wet. When the ball has risen to the surface of the water, scoop it out and gather the two doughs together into one cohesive ball, kneading as little as possible. When they are well blended, roll the ball into a cylinder about 2″ in diameter. With a sharp knife cut off muffins about ½″ to ¾″ thick. Dust one side with flour and set that end on a baking sheet. Make an indentation on the top of the muffins and dribble a little of the fat in each dent. Bake in a preheated oven of 400° for 35 minutes. Serve while hot.

FRESH RASPBERRIES WITH CRÈME ANGLAIS

2 pts. raspberries
½ cup milk
½ cup cream
4 egg yolks
¼ cup sugar
⅛ tsp. salt
1 tbsp. framboise

Whisk together the yolks, salt and sugar. Combine the milk and cream and whisk that into the yolks. Cook over a medium-high heat stirring constantly until it thickens quite suddenly. Remove from the heat, strain and then whisk until cool. Add the liqueur and spoon the creme anglais over the raspberries. Can be served hot or cold.

Offshore Saltwater Fish

W e fished in a tournament once and really thought it was terrific fun. It was a bluefish tournament for Grady White boats. We fished over an August weekend off the coast of Lynn, Massachusetts and were trying to catch the biggest bluefish or the smallest bluefish or the best combined weight over the two days. We caught a shark. Not a mako shark, just a little dogfish shark. This was quite exciting to our hosts who explained that in England (where they were born) "fish and chips" were made out of this type of fish. It was boneless and absolutely delicious.

We did actually catch some bluefish, too. Not enough to win the tournament but enough to learn a few things. In the last hour of the tournament I was beginning to see a great correlation between the number of fish caught, and when the gin and tonics started to be served; also between the size of the fish caught and the number of gin and tonics drunk. At the time, that correlation was very clear, but I can't remember it now. The correlation I do remember concerned the care of the fish once caught. Because we were trying to keep the weight of the fish up, we avoided letting the fish bleed (no bonks on the head) and he was immediately iced. Even at this, the weight dropped dramatically (about 25%) from the time he was caught and weighed to the time he had travelled five hours to the dock and been weighed. In photographing fish, you find his colors the best and brightest before he dies. Certainly the taste must change as each hour passes, too.

71

Of course, the quality of flavor as it relates to the freshness of fish is not a particularly novel concept, just one that is uniquely within the fisherman's control and consequently should be managed properly. There is one interesting observation I can make about these big fish. With almost all meat and many freshwater fish, size and age of the animal has as much or more to do with the good flavor as does freshness. It seems that a large old buck whitetail is not nearly as tasty as the small tender antelope, or mutton versus spring lamb. This is not true with these large saltwater fish. A smaller tuna does not taste perceptibly better than one that weighs 75 pounds more. There may be a difference in bonito or tuna, but can it be said that one is better than the other? The consistency in the flavor of the big fish is one reason they are such a pleasure to cook. Barring six martinis before dinner and a burnt swordfish steak, there is virtually nothing that will change the great flavor that is already in the swordfish. It will not be tough or gamey or full of sinew, it is simply marvelous just the way it is.

Japanese Leftover Tuna
Sautéed Watercress
Melon and Fortune Cookies

Serves four

Fortune cookies, of course, cannot be made by us.

JAPANESE LEFTOVER TUNA

Leftover cooked tuna—as much as you have. If little, add more of the rest of the ingredients; if a lot, decrease ingredients.

1 bag imported Japanese pasta (called soba). Available in gourmet and health food stores (a buckwheat pasta).
3 cans water chestnuts, drained and sliced
Sesame oil
Soy sauce
Ponzu sauce or similar sauce

There are many sauces (*tsuyu, kake, jiru,* etc.), hot and not so hot, and if what you want is unavailable, ask your grocer to order it.

Break up the tuna into small pieces. Season with pepper and soy. Sauté the water chestnuts in sesame oil and set aside. Cook pasta in water according to directions and then season with sesame oil, soy, and other seasoning. Toss with fish.

SAUTÉED WATERCRESS

3 bunches of watercress
3-4 tbsp. unsalted butter
Salt and pepper

Take each bunch of watercress and cut into 2″ lengths (the bunches should be cut approximately into thirds). Sauté the watercress in the hot butter for a second or two, then add the lid for two minutes. Remove the lid, season with salt and pepper and a little more butter and serve.

Fresh Tuna Steaks
Pizza
Nice Green Salad
Blueberries with Crème Anglais

Serves four

Fresh tuna is one of the great fish; go out of your way to obtain some. This goes for fresh mozzarella as well. It is really a different cheese from the mozzarella you get in the plastic bags in the supermarket (this is true also of Parmesan cheese) and fresh mozzarella will make your pizza exceptional. See page 214 for a nice green salad.

FRESH TUNA STEAKS

2 lbs. fresh tuna steaks
  Any of the compound butters
    you still have in the
    refrigerator, especially red
    pepper butter (p. 80) or
    lemon and garlic butter (p.
    83).

Grill the steaks about 6 minutes on the first side, 5 on the second. Just before the steaks are done, put some of the butter on each steak and then again when you are just about to serve it.

PIZZA

- 1 package dry yeast
- 1⅓ cups lukewarm water
- 3 cups all-purpose flour
- 1 tsp. salt
- 1 tsp. dried thyme
  Oil and cornmeal
- 4-6 tomatoes, peeled, seeded and sliced
- 3-4 tbsp. good Italian olive oil
  Salt and pepper—fresh ground or red flakes
- 2 tbsp. basil, roughly chopped
- ⅔-¾ cup mozzarella, grated—fresh if possible. If fresh, thin slices are fine.

In a small bowl add the warm water to the yeast. Stir and let stand for 10 minutes. In a large bowl combine flour, thyme and salt. Make a well in the center and add the yeast and water. Stir well to mix and form the dough. Turn out onto a lightly floured board and knead well for about 5 minutes. The dough will have become smooth and elastic. Place the dough in a large bowl coated with oil. Cover tightly with plastic wrap and let rise for about 1½ hours or until doubled in bulk. Divide the dough into 4 pieces. Roll out into thin circles and set on cookie sheets sprinkled liberally with flour. Put your toppings on. If you use fresh mozzarella, put the cheese on first, then the basil, then the tomatoes, then the pepper and olive oil. Bake in a pre-heated 450° oven. If possible, have tiles on the bottom shelf of the oven preheated for 30 minutes. Sprinkle with cornmeal just before cooking and slide the pizzas onto the tiles. Bake 15 minutes and sprinkle with salt and serve.

BLUEBERRIES WITH CRÈME ANGLAIS

        4 cups blueberries, washed and
             picked over
     ½ cup milk
     ½ cup heavy cream
        4 yolks
     ¼ cup sugar
     ⅛ tsp. salt
        1 tbsp. liqueur or vanilla (Grand
             Marnier is good)

    Whisk together the salt, yolks and sugar. Combine the milk and cream and whisk that into the yolks. Cook over a medium-high heat stirring constantly until it thickens quite suddenly. Remove from the heat, strain and then whisk until cool. Add the liqueur or vanilla and spoon the crème anglais over the blueberries and serve.

Fried Pasta with Water Chestnuts
Grilled Tuna with Lemon Butter
Salad of Melon, Pears and Cucumbers

Serves four

I discovered to my horror that good oils can go rancid. This seems to be particularly true of the more delicate oils such as hazelnut or walnut oil. Keeping them in the refrigerator is one solution, or splitting the oil and the cost with a friend so there isn't as much to use up is another solution.

FRIED PASTA WITH WATER CHESTNUTS

½ lb. pasta, bows or farfalle are
    nice
¼ cup toasted sesame oil, splash of
    vegetable oil
¼ cup soy sauce
2-3 tbsp. ginger, peeled and
    julienned into match sticks
2 garlic cloves, finely chopped
¼ cup rice wine vinegar
2 cans water chestnuts, drained
    and sliced
4 scallions, julienned and blanched
    for 30 seconds in boiling
    water, then plunged into ice
    water and drained

Cook the pasta until just *al dente*. Drain well. Toss with a little of the sesame oil so the bows won't stick together and set aside. Heat in a frying pan ¼ cup of sesame oil with a splash of vegetable oil till hot. Add the garlic and ginger and stir for a few minutes. Add the pasta and fry it till the edges start to crisp. Now add the soy sauce and the rice vinegar a little at a time over the fried pasta, tasting the pasta as you add. One day you may want more soy, the next more vinegar. You may also want to add more sesame oil. Add salt and pepper as well to taste. Toss in the water chestnuts and fry a little more. Now add the scallions, toss and serve.

GRILLED TUNA WITH LEMON BUTTER

4 tuna steaks at least 1″ thick,
  about 8-10 oz. each
Oil to paint the fish
Several sprigs of rosemary
1 stick of unsalted butter, softened
2 tsp. lemon juice
1 tsp. lemon rind, grated
½ tsp. dry mustard
1 tsp. butter
Salt and pepper

Whip the butter till fluffy. Add juice, rind, mustard and salt and pepper. Whip till mixed well, then mound onto plastic wrap and roll into a cylinder. Freeze a night ahead then bring into the refrigerator a few hours before serving. Brush the steaks with oil and lay the sprigs of rosemary on the coals as you put the steaks on. Grill until done, about 7 minutes on the first side and 4 on the second. Remove to a platter and sprinkle with salt and pepper. Top with pats of the lemon butter.

SALAD OF MELON, PEARS, AND CUCUMBERS

½ cup hazelnuts, toasted and
  chopped coarsely
4 pears
2 medium sized cucumbers
1 small melon
Lemon juice
1 tsp. mustard
2 tbsp. red wine vinegar
½ cup hazelnut or walnut oil
Salt and pepper

Combine the vinegar, mustard, oil and salt and pepper in the blender. Turn on high for a couple of seconds and then set aside. Toast the hazelnuts in the oven set at 300°. Remove and cover with a towel for 5 or 10 minutes, then rub off the skins and chop coarsely. Peel, core, and slice the pears and toss with a little lemon juice. Add slices of melon, about an equal amount to the pears. Peel, seed, and slice the cucumbers. Toss the cucumbers, pears and melon together with the vinaigrette and let sit an hour or so. Just before serving toss in the toasted hazelnuts.

Grilled Swordfish with Roasted Red Pepper Butter
Green and Purple Cole Slaw
Grilled Idahos
Summer Trifle

Serves four

Yes, this chapter on swordfish suggests only one way to cook swordfish. Grilling is the best way to cook swordfish and suggesting any other technique would be implying that other techniques might be good. There is only one way to cook swordfish and that is to grill it. It is too expensive and too difficult to catch to fool with other techniques. Go with the best.

GRILLED SWORDFISH WITH ROASTED RED PEPPER BUTTER

> 2 small red peppers
> 1½ sticks or 6 oz. of unsalted, room
> temperature butter
> Salt and pepper
> Small spot of Worcestershire
> sauce
> 2 lbs. swordfish
> Good olive oil for basting

Prepare the butter in advance. On a hot grill, roast whole red peppers until blackened on all sides. Remove to a plate and when cool enough to handle, peel off all the skin. Slice open and clean out all membrane and seeds. Chop roughly and purée in food processor. Season with salt and pepper. With electric mixer, whip butter until light and fluffy. Add pepper purée in small batches to see how much the butter can hold. You want to add as much as you can, but it will depend on how big the peppers are. When you feel it is right, taste, season with salt and pepper, and just a little dash of Worcestershire. Mix well. Mound onto plastic wrap and mold into a cylinder. Freeze for 24 hours and then bring to refrigerator several hours before using.

Baste the swordfish with olive oil and grill on a preheated grill.

Slice the compound butter in ¼ " slices and give several per portion. I say just slather it on!

GREEN AND PURPLE COLE SLAW

          3 cups finely shredded green savoy
              cabbage
          3 cups finely shredded purple
              cabbage
          1 large carrot, grated
          ½ tsp. salt
          2 tsp. prepared mustard
          ¼ tsp. ground pepper
          1 dash cayenne
          3 egg yolks
          2 cups corn oil or good olive oil
          1 tsp. salt
          ¼ cup vinegar
          2 tsp. sugar
          ¼ cup sour cream
          2 tsp. lemon juice
          2 tsp. caraway seeds
          1 tbsp. dry mustard

Keep the cabbages separate. Divide the carrot between them.

Now make a mayonnaise by combining in a bowl: ½ teaspoon salt, the prepared mustard, pepper, and cayenne. Let the salt melt and add the egg yolks. Whisk until frothy and well combined. Add the oil slowly in a dribble until the mayonnaise begins to take and thicken. Then you may add the oil faster. When finished, taste for seasoning and adjust. Add a tablespoon of hot water to finish it off. This also can be made in a food processor. Now add the remaining ingredients to the mayonnaise and divide between the two cabbages. Be sure to dissolve the salt in vinegar first as it will not dissolve well in the mayonnaise. Mix well and taste for seasoning. You will want a nice sweet sour taste. Grate a little black pepper over each and chill for several hours. Mix again before serving.

GRILLED IDAHOS

3 Idaho potatoes, sliced lengthwise
1 cup good olive oil
8 peeled garlic cloves
1½ tsp. thyme
1 bay leaf

Heat on low heat all the ingredients (but the potatoes) for 20-30 minutes. Remove garlic. (The softened garlic can now be used for whatever
your taste buds tell you, i.e. smearing on the potatoes or on the swordfish
before you add the red pepper butter or for the cook to halve atop a piece of
French bread.) Baste the potato slices with olive basting oil and grill also.
Season with salt and pepper just before serving.

SUMMER TRIFLE

1 sponge cake (store-bought is
  okay)
5 egg yolks
2 cups light cream
½ cup sugar
  Framboise or rum
  Raspberries
  Raspberry jam—optional
  Pinch of salt

Make a custard by mixing cream, yolks, sugar, and salt together in heavy
saucepan. Over a medium-high heat, stir the mixture constantly until it
thickens (which it will do quite suddenly, just as a cloud of steam rises from
the surface). Remove from heat and pour through fine strainer into bowl and
whisk to stop cooking. Cool, stirring occasionally and add framboise to taste.

In your best glass bowl put a layer of sponge cake with jam on it if you
like. Spoon in cool custard just to cover. Spread profusely with raspberries
(grate on a little orange rind if you like). Add more cake, then more custard,
and finish with raspberries. Be sure the berries of each layer show off in an
orderly manner through the glass. Chill overnight.

Grilled Swordfish with Garlic Butter
Panzanella Salad
Strawberry Sherbet

Serves four

When we call for good olive oil in a recipe, this is not done casually. There are terrific differences in olive oils. It is much like wine, and like wine, quality should be matched to the usage and occasion. For everyday salad use, I use everyday olive oil. But when the queen comes to lunch, it better be a good green virgin olive oil. And when you are going to baste a swordfish steak it better be good oil.

GRILLED SWORDFISH WITH GARLIC BUTTER

          1 or 2 swordfish steaks (depending
             on size)
             Good olive oil for basting
       1½ sticks unsalted butter
          2 tsp. chopped garlic
          1 tsp. lemon rind, grated
             Salt and pepper

At least 24 hours before, prepare the compound butter. Whip the butter till fluffy, then add the garlic, lemon rind and salt and pepper to taste. Mound onto a piece of plastic wrap and shape into a cylinder. Place in the freezer the day before, then take out and bring to room temperature just before serving.

Paint the swordfish with a good olive oil, then grill. Serve with generous amounts of garlic butter on each serving.

PANZANELLA SALAD

    8 thick slices day-old Italian or
         French bread
  ½ cup stock
    3 tbsp. butter
    2 tomatoes, peeled, seeded, and
         coarsely chopped
    1 medium cucumber, seeded and
         chopped
    1 small red onion, chopped
    1 head romaine lettuce
       A few bitter greens, such as
         chicory or escarole
       Shredded fresh basil leaves
       A good vinaigrette—your own,
         or see page 210
       Salt and pepper

Cut the bread into large cubes and dribble the stock over them. Fry in butter until crisp and let cool. Combine all remaining ingredients and toss with the vinaigrette. Check for salt and pepper and let sit a little before serving, to meld the flavors.

STRAWBERRY SHERBET

    1 cup sugar
  ½ cup water
       Squeeze of lemon juice
       Tiny pinch of salt
    1 qt. ripe strawberries, hulled
       Dash of framboise or white rum

Combine the sugar and water and bring to a boil. Let boil for five minutes, then cool. Purée the fruit and add the salt, lemon juice and framboise. Add the sugar water, tasting as you go. You may not need all of the sugar syrup. Add a few whole berries and chill. Follow your ice cream maker's directions. Serve with cookies.

Corn Chowder
Grilled Swordfish Steaks
Grilled Artichokes
Apricot Ice

Serves four

If you have access to the little tiny artichokes (we find them in Boston's Italian North End in the Spring and they are available in parts of California, too) they would be good to use in this recipe.

CORN CHOWDER

2½ cups cooked corn
1 large onion, chopped fine
1 small rib celery, chopped fine
1 large green pepper, diced
2 or 3 potatoes, peeled and diced
1 tbsp. bacon fat
6 tbsp. unsalted butter
2 qts. light cream
½ bay leaf
  Pinch basil
  Salt and pepper

Sauté the onion and celery until translucent. Add potatoes and green pepper. Toss in fat and butter and add light cream. Add bay leaf, some salt and pepper and a pinch of basil. Let simmer until potatoes are done, approximately 30 minutes. Add 2½ cups corn and taste for seasoning.

If you should wish to have a thicker soup, just before serving: Mix 4 tablespoons cornstarch with ⅔ cup soup. Stir and add mixture back into the hot soup. Stir gently. Bring to a boil and serve.

Garnish each soup plate first with:

¼ lb. cooked ham, diced and
    sautéed and divided among
    the plates
  Some finely chopped pimento

Sprinkle the top of the soup with chopped parsley.

GRILLED SWORDFISH STEAKS

4 good-sized swordfish steaks

Baste with olive oil or butter and a few grinds pepper. Grill on a pre-heated grill. Serve with lemon wedges and melted butter; reserve some for the artichokes as well.

GRILLED ARTICHOKES

4 large artichokes
Olive oil

Trim stem of artichokes to ½ ". Slice off the tops with a knife and then with a scissors cut off each sharp thorn, about ⅛-¼ of the leaf. Steam for 30-45 minutes. They are done when a leaf pulls off easily, and you want them to be done. When cool enough to handle, cut into quarters and remove the choke. Paint with olive oil and grill to desired brownness.

APRICOT ICE

4 17-oz. cans of apricot halves in
      heavy syrup. Drain well and
      reserve the syrup.
2 medium size lemons for the
      juice
   Splash of white rum (1 tbsp.)
   Pinch of salt

Purée the apricots in a food processor. Add a pinch of salt, ¾ of all the lemon juice, the rum and about ⅔ cup of the apricot syrup. Taste for balance. You may want more sweetness (syrup) or tartness (lemon juice) or rum. Prepare as your ice cream machine says for ice. Remember you use less salt than for ice cream. Decorate with fresh mint if you like or a pint of fresh raspberries.

Kingfish with Lime Butter
Banana Chips
Tomatoes, Red and Green Peppers
Potato Cake
Real Tuttifrutti

Serves four

KINGFISH WITH LIME BUTTER

1½ lbs. kingfish
1½ sticks of unsalted butter
  2 shallots, chopped very fine
  1 clove garlic, chopped very fine
     Grated rind of 2 limes
     Salt and pepper

The lime butter should be in readiness in your freezer for the happy moment when the fisherman comes home. So at least 24 hours before you expect the fish to arrive, whip the butter until fluffy and white. Add the shallots, lime rind, garlic, and salt and pepper and mix well. Check the taste and add more salt and pepper if necessary. Turn out onto a piece of plastic wrap, wrap it up and shape into a log. Freeze it, making sure it goes into the refrigerator one hour before serving.

Fillet the kingfish, leaving the skin on one side. Each fillet should be no more than an inch thick. Grill over charcoal a few minutes on each side. Remove from the grill and put pats of the lime butter on top.

BANANA CHIPS

3 or 4 medium-green bananas (about 1
lb.)
2½ inches of corn oil or peanut oil

Slice the bananas either lengthwise or across, whatever is your fancy, so
the chips are ⅛″ thick. Heat the oil till it is 375° and fry a few pieces of
banana at a time for about four minutes. Make sure you turn them once
during the cooking. They should be a nice golden brown when done. Remove to drain on paper towels. Serve with your favorite tropical drink.

TOMATOES, RED AND GREEN PEPPERS

2 tomatoes, very ripe, seeded and
julienned
2 green peppers, seeded and
julienned
2 red peppers, seeded and
julienned
2 yellow peppers, seeded and
julienned
Olive oil
Fresh coriander or chopped
parsley
Salt and pepper

Splash a bit of the olive oil in two frying pans and sauté the red peppers
in one pan and the green and yellow peppers in the other. Sauté until they
are just done and still a little crunchy. Add some of the tomatoes to each pan
along with the coriander and heat through. Season with salt and pepper. You
can stir them all together now or arrange in an attractive pattern on a serving
platter.

POTATO CAKE

2 lbs. all-purpose potatoes
2-5 tbsp. corn oil
2 tbsp. unsalted butter
1 freshly grated nutmeg
Salt and pepper

Peel and slice the potatoes very thin, about $\frac{1}{16}$" thick. You can use a food processor for this if you like. Keep the slices in ice water until you're ready to use them, then rinse under cold water and dry on a kitchen towel. Heat half of the oil in a 10"-12" skillet. Add the potatoes and sauté until lightly brown all over, about 10 minutes. Season with the grated nutmeg and salt and pepper. Stir again. Press the potatoes with a spatula or spoon into a flat layer in the pan and cook 5 more minutes, shaking the pan every now and then. Then invert the potato cake onto a lightly oiled plate and add the other half of the oil to the pan. Return the potato cake to the pan with the unbrowned side down. Finish cooking, about 5 to 10 minutes more, or until potatoes are completely brown but tender. Slide cake onto a platter and spread soft butter on top.

REAL TUTTIFRUTTI

2 oranges
2 grapefruits
½ pineapple
1 papaya
1 banana
8 tbsp. orange liqueur

Cut the ends off the grapefruit and oranges and stand on end. Then with a sharp knife cut off the remaining peel. Separate into sections making sure the connecting tissue is left behind. Core and pare the pineapple half and cut into small pieces. Core, pare and seed the papaya and cut into small pieces. Slice the banana. In a bowl combine all of the fruit and sprinkle the orange liqueur over it. Let it marinate in the refrigerator several hours. Serve garnished with mint.

Rice and Parsley Soup
Mako Shark Steaks with Lemon Dill
Green Beans with Sesame Seeds
Sauterne

Serves four

RICE AND PARSLEY SOUP

4 vegetable or chicken bouillon
  cubes
6 tbsp. unsalted butter
1 small onion, chopped
5 tbsp. chopped parsley
4 Idaho potatoes (baking),
  parboiled for 15 minutes, then
  grated through the round
  holes of a grater
2 qts. water
¾ cup uncooked rice—Italian is
  best, but regular okay
1 tsp. salt
¼ tsp. fresh ground pepper
  Fresh nutmeg
1½ cups Parmesan cheese

Melt 3 tablespoons of the butter. Cook the onion until translucent over medium heat and continue cooking until just starting to turn golden. Then add potatoes, water, salt, pepper, a few grates of nutmeg, bouillon cubes and half of the parsley. Bring slowly to a boil and add rice. Cover and lower heat until rice is just cooked *al dente*—about 20 minutes. Give one or two quick grinds in food processor if you like. Correct seasoning. Add butter, cheese and remaining parsley.

MAKO SHARK STEAKS WITH LEMON DILL BUTTER

4 good-sized shark steaks, 1″ thick
1½ sticks of unsalted butter at room
    temperature
2 tsp. dried dill, revived in a little
    hot water
    Salt and pepper
1 tsp. grated lemon rind
1 tsp. lemon juice
    Pinch of cayenne pepper
    Flour for dusting

In advance, whip 1 stick of butter until fluffy. Add the dill, lemon juice, lemon rind, cayenne, salt and pepper. Whip until well mixed and then turn out onto plastic wrap and roll up like a small log. Freeze for 24 hours. Bring to refrigerator a few hours before using.

Dry steaks with paper towels. Season lightly with salt and pepper and dust lightly with flour, shaking off excess. Heat 4 tablespoons sweet butter over medium high heat until sizzling. Add steaks and cook 8 minutes first side and 6-8 minutes the second side. They should be nice and golden brown. Place on warm plates or platter and top with ½″ slices of the compound butter. Let sit a few seconds so the butter starts to melt before serving or run under the broiler.

GREEN BEANS WITH SESAME SEEDS

1½ lbs. green beans, ends removed
    (If beans are quite long, cut in
    half on the diagonal.)
1½ tbsp. sesame seeds
3-4 tbsp. unsalted butter
    Salt and pepper

Blanch the beans until *al dente* in a large quantity of boiling salted water. Refresh in ice water and drain. This may be done several hours before serving time and then wrap the beans in a dish towel and refrigerate. Toast sesame seeds on medium heat in a heavy skillet. Just as they start to turn a golden color remove from the heat and transfer to a plate or bowl. Just before serving time, melt the sweet butter until hot. Sauté the beans, stirring until heated through. Add sesame seeds, season with salt and pepper. Toss and serve.

Capered Dolphin
Red, Green and Yellow Pepper Salad
Sweet Pastry with Jam

Serves four

CAPERED DOLPHIN

1½-2 lbs. dolphin fillets
1½ tbsp. chopped capers (the big
        ones are best), well rinsed first
        if salted
1 large clove garlic, chopped
1 tsp. grated lemon rind
1½ sticks unsalted butter
    Salt and pepper
1 tsp. finely chopped parsley

In advance make the compound butter. Whip the butter until light and fluffy. Add salt and pepper, garlic, lemon rind, capers and parsley. Mix well and mound onto plastic wrap. Form into a cylinder and freeze for 24 hours. Bring to room temperature before using.

Broil the dolphin for about 10 minutes (depending on thickness of steaks) and put a little of the caper butter on top ⅔ of the way through.

RED, GREEN, AND YELLOW PEPPER SALAD

3 large peppers of each color,
  cored, seeded, julienned and
  the red peppers kept separate
  from the yellow and green
3 tbsp. corn oil or olive
⅓ cup red wine vinegar or balsamic
  vinegar

Salt and pepper
1 tsp. prepared mustard
2 shallots, chopped very fine
1 tbsp. dried tarragon, revived in a
  little hot water
⅔ cup good olive oil, added last

Sauté peppers, yellow and green together, red separately in olive or corn oil until just *al dente*. Season with salt and pepper and toss with a dressing made from the remaining ingredients. Blend dressing well. Toss peppers altogether and serve at room temperature.

SWEET PASTRY WITH JAM

½ cup unsalted butter
⅓ cup sugar
  Pinch of salt
2-3 eggs
1 tsp. baking powder
1 cup all purpose flour
½ cup corn flour
1 tsp. grated lemon rind
1 jar of jam

Cream butter and add sugar, salt, lemon rind and 1 egg. Mix well. Mix flour, corn flour and baking powder together and add to the butter mixture by flattening it against the side of the bowl with a large spatula, sort of squeezing it into the butter and sugar and then flatten and shape into a cake shape. Wrap dough in plastic wrap and chill for several hours. Roll out dough to ¼"-⅜" thickness on a floured surface. If it is too difficult, roll between waxed paper. Chill and then remove the waxed paper for the cutting. Cut 3" to 4" ovals, squares, etc. Gather scraps and reroll to get as many cookies as possible. Paint the surface of each piece with thin layer of beaten egg (you may need 2 whole eggs to do all). Spoon a tablespoon or so of jam (apricot or raspberry jam are good classics, but try fig, marmalade, etc.) in the center of the dough. Fold it over and seal by pushing down with the tines of a fork around the edges excluding the folded edge. Now paint the tops with beaten egg. Place cookies on buttered baking sheets. Bake in preheated 350° oven until golden, about 20 minutes. Cool on racks. You will be surprised how many of these little delectables people can eat.

Pina Coladas
Banana Chips
Wahoo Steaks Shish Kebab
White Rice
Grilled Pineapple with Orange Ice

Serves four

See page 88 for Banana Chips recipe. You know how to make white rice.

WAHOO STEAKS SHISH KEBAB

         4 good-sized steaks, 1½″ thick, cut
            into squares
         1 green pepper, in pieces
         2 sweet red peppers, cut in large
            pieces
         1 large sweet onion, cubed
      8-12 firm cherry tomatoes
        1½ tbsp. dried oregano,
            reconstituted
         ½ to ⅔ cup olive oil
            Juice of 1 lemon
            A pinch each of salt and pepper
         ¼ tsp. chopped garlic

Combine oregano, oil, lemon juice, salt, pepper and garlic and marinate fish cubes for several hours. Assemble shish kebabs, putting cherry tomatoes on last. Grill, turning once. Paint with marinade; serve with white rice. Also, these steaks may be served with any of the compound butter sauces listed with other firm-fleshed fish steaks.

GRILLED PINEAPPLE WITH ORANGE ICE

> 1 fresh pineapple skinned, cored
>   and cut into 1″ slices
> 1 pint orange ice
>   Sprinkles of Grand Marnier

Sprinkle the pineapple slices with Grand Marnier and grill quickly until hot and slightly browned. Lay on a plate and top each slice with a scoop of orange ice.

Fish From the Tropics

I have fished now quite a few times in tropical places. And I've caught very few fish. I've not been sorry for that.

There was the time in Jamaica with Ed and Patrick and Marcie when we went up the Black River looking for tarpon and saw a large swirl created by a very large tail but nothing more. There was the time in Tortola when a friend of mine threw his fishing gear, tackle bag and all, into a wave on an outgoing tide. Frustration, I guess, at the wiliness of the fish. There was the time when I was twelve out in front of my grandparents' house on the Gulf of Mexico with my brother and sister and grandfather when even shrimp wouldn't catch them. And then, most recently, on Green Turtle Cay, when it was too windy for me to even attempt a bit of fly casting.

But I've never really been sorry for the absence of fish in those places. Maybe I hark back to my first time saltwater fishing. About eight years old, I remember standing on some coral rocks casting out to sea at dusk and cranking back, endlessly casting and cranking, casting and cranking with the odd tug here or nibble there. What was that! I would follow that line down to where it disappeared into the water and think about the bait (or plug or fly) dancing along flashing in front of fish, lots of fish, and fantasize about what would finally grab the hook. The fantasy played along so extravagantly and with such great mystery that I think I forgot that I wasn't catching fish—and I'm sure I was happier for it. Many times since, my mind has made that trip to the Bahamas, sometimes while fishing and sometimes while not. And although I can think of no better fish to eat than pompano or snapper, I think I prefer the slow, sweet, magical tropics with no fish to eat—just fantasies.

But in case you must come back to reality, these menus will help.

Grilled Pompano with Mint and Orange Rind
Brown Rice with Pignoli Nuts and Green Beans
Your Nice Green Salad
Sauterne and Sugar Cookies

Serves four

Pignoli nuts, or pine nuts as they are called in English, are a perfectly wonderful nut to add to boring vegetables and should probably be kept on hand at all times. Madame Cintra demands that all nuts be cooked (roasted or sautéed) if they are used in a recipe. This is a common demand of real cooks. A word of caution, pignoli nuts burn quite easily if you try to roast them. Sauté them, as they are expensive, and avoid the risk of burning them.

Serve a mild green salad with no bitter greens and sauterne and sugar cookies for dessert. (See page 30 for recipe.)

GRILLED POMPANO WITH MINT AND ORANGE RIND

1 lb. pompano fillets, skin
    removed
1½ sticks unsalted butter
2 tbsp. dried mint, revived
    Grated rind of 1 orange
    Dash of Tabasco sauce
    Salt and fresh ground pepper to
    taste

Reconstitute the mint in warm water. Whip the butter until light and fluffy. Add salt and pepper, grated orange rind, Tabasco and mint. Mix well and mound onto plastic wrap. Form into a cylinder and freeze for 24 hours. Bring to room temperature before using. Grill the pompano a few minutes on each side.

Just before done, put a few pats of the butter on the fish and add some more after.

BROWN RICE WITH PIGNOLI NUTS AND GREEN BEANS

1 cup brown rice
¼ cup pignoli nuts
½ lb. green beans
1 tbsp. salt
    Salt, pepper and noisette butter
    to taste

Bring 2¼ cups water to a boil and add the salt and rice. Cover and reduce heat and cook until tender, about 30 to 45 minutes. Sauté the pignoli nuts in 1 tablespoon unsalted butter until golden brown. Mix together the rice and nuts and add the green beans which you've cut on the diagonal into ½" pieces and blanched for 1 minute. Add salt and pepper and a little noisette butter, about 2 to 3 tablespoons.

Grilled Red Snapper with Lime Butter Sauce and Grilled Pineapple
Bibb Salad
Cornbread
Coconut Ice Cream

Serves four

Ice cream is very satisfying to make at home even when you live, as we do, in the state that has more ice cream parlors than any other. In Massachusetts it is very easy to get fresh, homemade ice cream. I do not think it is worthwhile to either crank by hand or spend a lot of money on a fancy ice cream maker. The extremes are unnecessary. Just buy a $30 electric machine; that will do the job nicely.

GRILLED RED SNAPPER WITH LIME BUTTER SAUCE AND GRILLED PINEAPPLE

4 fillets of red snapper
8 very thin slices of pineapple,
    peeled and cored
Rind of one lime (Peel with
    potato peeler, being sure to
    remove only the green rind
    and none of the white pith.
    Cut into pieces the size of
    matchsticks and blanch in
    boiling water for 2 minutes.)
2 tbsp. vinegar
2 shallots, chopped fine and
    sautéed in butter
¼ cup white wine
8 oz. plus a tbsp. (for sautéing the
    shallots) unsalted butter
Salt and pepper

Combine the 2 tablespoons vinegar, wine, salt and pepper with the cooked shallots and reduce by ½ to ⅔. Now with the vinegar wine reduction at a hot but not boiling temperature, add the butter in small bits, whisking constantly. The sauce will become foamy and white. Paint the fish and the pineapple lightly with the butter sauce. Put the pineapple on the grill a little before the fish. You will want it chewy and lightly caramelized. Grill fish until done. Put the remaining butter sauce under the fish on the plate with the pineapple around. Sprinkle a little of the lime rind on top.

BIBB SALAD

4 heads Bibb lettuce, cleaned
A few snips of chive
2 tbsp. red wine vinegar
½ cup good olive oil
1 tsp. prepared mustard
Salt and pepper

Combine vinegar, oil, mustard, and salt and pepper in a blender and zip on high for a second or two. Toss with the lettuce and chives.

CORNBREAD

1½ cups cornmeal
2 tsp. baking powder
1 tsp. salt
¼ cup flour
2 tbsp. sugar
2 tbsp. unsalted butter
2 eggs
1 cup buttermilk
3 tbsp. bacon drippings
1 tbsp. finely diced sweet red
    pepper

Sift together the cornmeal, baking powder, salt, sugar and flour. Sauté the red pepper in the bacon fat. Beat the eggs, add the buttermilk and red pepper along with the bacon drippings. Now combine this with the dry ingredients. Bake in a 425° oven for 15 to 25 minutes (depending on whether you cook the corn bread in corn stick molds or muffin tins.)

COCONUT ICE CREAM

1 cup grated coconut
2 cups whole milk
1 cup granulated sugar
6 egg yolks
1 cup heavy cream, chilled
1 tbsp. coconut liqueur (a coconut
    flavored rum or white rum)

Bring the milk, ½ cup of the sugar and the coconut to a boil. Just as it boils, remove from the heat. Cover pot and let rest until cool.

Combine the egg yolks and the other ½ cup sugar and mix with whisk or electric beater until thick and creamy. Add the cooled coconut milk to the egg yolk mixture. Mix well. Return to heat in heavy-bottomed saucepan, and over medium heat stirring constantly, cook until it thickens, which it will do quite suddenly (between 5-10 minutes). Pour into a large bowl and stir for a few minutes to stop cooking. Add the heavy cream, the liqueur and stir well to mix. Chill mixture well, stirring from time to time. Make according to your ice cream machine's directions. Serve with chocolate cookies.

Saltwater Bottom Fish

O ne of the greatest aspects of saltwater fishing is that, more than any other place, in the ocean a fisherman can be surprised by what he catches. How many times have we all gone out for bluefish and returned home with flounder? Sometimes this is a result of needing to be versatile with fishing methods, sometimes the surprise happens as we're reeling in. It sure does seem sometimes that flounder will just jump onto your hook saying, "Take me, eat me, I'm yours."

Too many times we as fishermen are disappointed with catching something different from what we set out to catch. In Alaska the exclamation, "A grayling, oh no, where's the rainbow!" has been heard more than once. And certainly in Gloucester Harbor there have been times when it seemed like my fellow fisherman was almost literally shaking his rod trying to get that flounder off the hook. Better to look at that fish as something to eat and cook, than as an unexpected intruder onto your hook.

The three fish in this chapter are often considered such intruders. Perhaps because they are so plentiful and relatively easy to catch, they are also sometimes a bit disappointing to catch. But since all three are delightfully flavored fish and are best tasting when absolutely fresh, as fresh as only a fisherman can make them, then you must approach them from a cook's vantage. Their frequency and occasionally unexpected appearance make them ideal for testing new recipes. And although the menus listed here for cod, flounder and sea bass are well suited to them, any, yes any, of the other fish recipes will work. Rarely is there a recipe in the book that will not work well on some species of fish other than the one it calls for. To determine applicability of one fish recipe to another kind of fish, consider the type of fish it is listed for. A recipe for a nice delicate brook trout will work well also on smallmouth bass. Went out for striper and came home with weakfish? Use the same recipe you were planning for striper on the weakfish. We have tried to group the fish by chapters according to likeness—not only likeness of habitat and species characteristics but also according to what recipes will work equally as well on all species within that chapter. In mixing species and menus be concerned mostly with matching the proper cooking technique with the size or proper cut. Grilled fillet of black-fin flounder will end up dripping onto the coals. This thoughtful improvisation in the kitchen is very similar to matching the hatch on the river and will breed the same success and feeling of satisfaction. It's worth catching a mess of flounder for that. Just find someone else to clean them!

Chinese Grilled Flounder with Noodles
Sautéed Watercress
Pear Sorbet with Fortune Cookies

Serves four

Sautéing greens was a revelation to me. Not only can it be done with watercress, but spinach and parsley. It's very tasty and easy and solves that age-old problem of what to do with the remaining bunch after you've used the three sprigs for garnish.

CHINESE GRILLED FLOUNDER

1½ lbs. flounder, skinned, trimmed
    and in 1″ pieces and put
    on grilling skewers
¼ cup corox oil
1 tbsp. lemon juice
2 tbsp. soy sauce
1 tbsp. rice wine vinegar
1 large garlic clove, chopped fine
1 piece ginger, peeled, chopped
    fine
1 shake red pepper flakes
1 tbsp. sesame oil
1 lb. oriental pasta
¼ cup peanuts or cashews, toasted
    in corn oil and coarsely
    chopped
3-6 scallions, green part only, cut
    into 1″ pieces
1 lb. mushrooms

Blend the oil, lemon juice, soy sauce, vinegar, garlic, ginger, and red pepper flakes in food processor, adding the corox oil last. Pour over fish, let rest several hours. Wrap the fish with the juices in foil and grill on a pre-heated grill, 2-3 minutes per side. Cook and drain the pasta and place the fish on top of it. Sauté the mushrooms quickly in the sesame oil. Remove from the heat and add the scallions and nuts. Season with salt and pepper. Top the fish with the nut and mushroom mixture and any leftover marinade.

SAUTÉED WATERCRESS

3 bunches watercress
3 tbsp. unsalted butter
   Salt and pepper

Take each bunch of watercress and cut into 2″ lengths (the bunches should be cut approximately into thirds). Sauté the watercress in the hot unsalted butter for a second or two and then add the lid for two minutes. Remove the lid, season with salt and pepper and a little more butter and serve.

PEAR SORBET

1 qt. ripe pears peeled, cored and
     puréed
1 cup sugar
1 cup water
2 tbsp. lemon juice
   A pinch of salt
1 tbsp. pear liqueur

Boil the water and sugar together 5 minutes. To puréed pears, add sugar syrup to taste, lemon juice to taste, a pinch of salt, and pear liqueur. Chill mixture, then freeze according to your ice cream machine's directions, but use less salt than recommended so ice crystals won't form. Serve with fortune cookies.

Gray Flounder
Sautéed Spinach
Fried Bread

Serves four

GRAY FLOUNDER

4 flounder fillets
2 large carrots or 8 tiny ones,
    julienned
3 sticks celery, julienned
1 potato, julienned
1 tbsp. orange rind, julienned and
    blanched for 30 seconds
1 tsp. garlic, finely minced
2 tbsp. unsalted butter
1½ cups heavy cream
1 tbsp. clam juice
   Salt and pepper

Sauté the vegetables, orange rind and garlic in the butter until just barely tender. Set aside. In a stove-to-table container, set some vegetables on the bottom of the dish. Arrange fish on top. Reduce the cream by boiling it in a frying pan until it is halved, then add the clam juice to the cream and whisk. Pour over the fish. Add the remaining vegetables on top of the fish—criss-cross or put in little bunches if you wish. Cook at a simmer uncovered for about 5 minutes. Season fish with salt and pepper and serve on heated plates.

SAUTÉED SPINACH

1 lb. spinach
2 tbsp. unsalted butter
Fresh grated nutmeg
Salt and pepper

Rinse and dry spinach. Remove stems and sauté in butter until just wilted. Season with salt and pepper and a few grates of fresh nutmeg.

FRIED BREAD

8 1″ slices of French or Italian
    bread
4 tbsp. unsalted butter
Salt and pepper
2 tbsp. fontina cheese, grated, or
    any cheese

Dry bread in oven at 300°. Fry in melted butter. Sprinkle with salt and pepper and cheese. Put back in oven to just melt.

Flounder and Scallop Soup
Fried Bread
Fig Tart

Serves four

Flounder and sea scallops have very much the same texture and taste. In fact, some restaurants take a cookie cutter to the flounder fillets and make them into very uniform looking scallops. So if you cannot get the small bay or Cape scallops or have caught an extraordinary number of flounder, just use all flounder in this recipe. The recipe for Fried Bread can be found on page 110.

FLOUNDER AND SCALLOP SOUP

For the Fumet of Fish:

3 cups of very good white wine
3-4 lbs. fish bones—preferably sole
   and flounder—heads included.
   Just remove the triangle of
   innards.
1 medium onion, chopped into
   pieces
1 very small carrot, sliced
4 parsley stems
10 peppercorns
   A few mushrooms
1 small bay leaf
   Pinch thyme
   Large pinch salt

This recipe will make about two quarts of stock. Please do not use an aluminum pot to make it in and please remember the better the wine, the better the soup. And with a nice fish stock you can put almost anything in the soup. Cook the onion, carrot, mushrooms and parsley stems in butter for 5-8 minutes. Add fish bones, cover pot, and let stew over low heat for a while until fish bones sort of collapse—about 10 minutes. Remove the lid and then add wine and 5 cups water. Bring to a boil and add salt, thyme, bay leaf and peppercorns. On medium heat, simmer for 30 minutes. Strain immediately. It should smell delicious and may be made a day ahead.

> 2 small zucchinis, julienned into
>   matchstick size pieces,
>   blanched
> 2 small yellow squash, julienned
>   into matchstick size pieces,
>   blanched
> 1 cup small broccoli florets,
>   blanched
> 1 pint scallops, sliced if necessary
> 2 or 3 fillets of flounder, chopped
>   into bite-size pieces

Taste fish stock and heat. Add scallops and cook for a few minutes until almost done. Add fish and vegetables. Cook for a few minutes more and season to taste and serve immediately.

A red wine fumet is also nice if using salmon or stronger types of fish.

FIG TART

> 18 green figs
> ½ cup rum
> 2 tbsp. honey
> 2 tbsp. unsalted butter
> 1 recipe short pastry or semi-puff
> 1 cup heavy cream
> 2 tsp. confectioners' sugar

Cook together the rum, honey and butter. Place figs in buttered dish and baste with the rum mixture. Cook at 350° until soft, but not too soft. The cooking time will vary depending on how ripe they are. Let cool. Roll out and line a buttered tart pan with pastry. Let sit 1 hour. Preheat oven to 425° for 20 minutes. Line pastry with tin foil and fill with beans or rice. Cook 5-7 minutes until set. Remove tin foil filled with beans and sprinkle tart with granulated sugar. Continue to cook another 5 minutes or so until the sugar starts to caramelize. Remove from oven and slip out of pan onto cooling rack. This can be done several hours ahead. Whip the cream with the confectioners' sugar. Add a little dash of rum if you like and spread on pastry. Arrange figs on top and brush with any leftover liquid. Serve immediately or within 1 hour.

Fish Chowder
Common Crackers
Green Salad
Gingerbread

Serves four

Cod is a wonderful fish if it is eaten very fresh; some people prefer it to haddock. It certainly is plentiful and caught easily by saltwater fishermen. Most of the recipes in this book would be appropriate to try on cod, but if you do not have a fresh cod or you have caught so much and had to freeze the fish this recipe is perfect to use.

FISH CHOWDER

1 8-lb. cod (approximately),
     cleaned and cut up
½ amount of potatoes as fish,
     peeled
1 qt. milk
1 can evaporated milk
½ pint all-purpose cream
½ lb. unsalted butter
   Salt and pepper
   Pinch thyme

Slice potatoes and put in kettle with some butter and a little water to cover. Bring to a boil and simmer about 10 minutes. Add cut up fish and salt and pepper to taste. Add more water to cover and a pinch of thyme and cook 30 minutes or until fish is tender. Stir in more butter and 1 can evaporated milk and cream. Add regular milk to obtain the fluid level you want. Taste for seasoning. Set aside and do not let boil again. Serve with fried salted pork and common crackers.

GINGERBREAD

½ cup unsalted butter
⅔ cup light brown sugar
1 egg
1½ cups all-purpose flour
½ cup boiling water
½ cup unsulphured molasses
1 tsp. baking soda
1¼ tsp. ground ginger
1 tsp. ground cinnamon
¾ tsp. ground cloves
1 cup heavy cream
Dash of rum
Confectioners' sugar

Preheat the oven to 350°. Butter a 13"×9"×2" baking pan. Put a piece of wax paper on the buttered bottom and butter that and dust with flour.

Whip butter until fluffy. Add sugar and mix well. Add egg and blend well. Sift flour with spices and baking soda and set aside. Combine molasses with boiling water. Alternately add flour mixture and water and molasses mixture to the butter, sugar, egg mixture. Pour batter into prepared baking pan and cook about 25-30 minutes or until cake tester comes out clean. Cool in pan on wire rack. Then remove from cake pan. This can be made ahead and stored for several days if tightly wrapped and kept at room temperature. Just before serving, dust with confectioners' sugar. Serve with lightly whipped cream and add a dash of rum to the cream.

Grilled Sea Bass with Sun-Dried Tomatoes, Pepper and Garlic
Straw Potato-Corn Cake
Your Nice Green Salad
Honey Ice Cream

Serves four

Sun-dried tomatoes have become a little bit more common an ingredient in recent years but still must be purchased from gourmet shops. My own taste dictates the purchase of the more expensive sun-dried tomatoes, the ones packed in olive oil, not the ones simply dried and salted. The salt is too over-bearing, and I like to use the oil in which the tomatoes have been packed in salad dressings and other recipes within the menu to "tie" the tastes together. When you make the vinaigrette for your salad in this menu (see the index or "Basics" chapter in this book if you can't think of a good salad on your own) use some of the oil from the sun-dried tomatoes.

GRILLED SEA BASS WITH SUN-DRIED TOMATOES, PEPPER AND GARLIC

1 3-pound sea bass, butterflied
(that is, skin left on, head and
tail removed) and boned and
split (remove scales)

1 sprig fresh basil or 1 tsp. dried

1 sprig fresh thyme or 1 tsp. dried

Salt and pepper

1 small onion, sliced finely

1 large green pepper, cored and
chopped into ½" pieces

2 cloves garlic, minced

½ cup olive oil

½ cup sun-dried tomatoes in oil,
roughly chopped (If they are
not in oil: in a small pot add
the tomatoes, 1 cup olive oil,
1 small clove garlic and a
pinch thyme. Heat until hot
and keep warm for 20 minutes
or until tomatoes have
plumped. Drain off oil and
reserve for another use. It's
great in salads.)

Dry fish and season with salt and pepper. Stuff with basil and thyme. Wrap tightly in foil and refrigerate for 2-4 hours. Preheat grill. Do not remove foil and cook 15 minutes one side and 12 the other. Test for doneness. While the fish is cooking or ahead of time make the sauce: Sauté onion in olive oil over medium-low heat until translucent. Add garlic, peppers and tomatoes. Cook until peppers are done to taste. Season with salt and pepper and a handful of chopped parsley. Let sit 20 minutes at least to meld flavors. Remove the herbs from the fish and spoon the sauce over it. Serve with a green salad.

STRAW POTATO-CORN CAKE

1½ lbs. baking potatoes
4 tbsp. unsalted butter
2 tbsp. oil
   Salt and pepper
   A 10″ teflon pan
6 tbsp. creamed corn

Peel potatoes, cut into ⅛″ slices and then into ⅛″ matchstick strips, or easier still, cut into matchstick juliennes in your food processor. Heat half the butter and all the oil until hot and add half the potatoes and spread around the center on top of the potatoes about 6 tablespoons cold creamed corn. Season with salt and pepper. Then add the rest of the potatoes. Season with salt and pepper and press down with spatula. Cook until the bottom is browned, by which time the whole cake will move as one. (Be sure you squish those potatoes down occasionally.) When the bottom is golden brown, lower the heat and cover and cook 7 minutes to cook the center of the cake. Remove cover and raise the heat. Flip the potato cake over and add a little more butter and brown the other side.

HONEY ICE CREAM

⅓ cup very aromatic and high
   quality honey
2 cups milk
6 egg yolks
⅔ cup sugar
1 cup heavy cream, chilled
   Crystalized lavender flowers for
      decoration (These can be
      purchased at a gourmet shop.)

Bring milk and honey slowly to the scalding point while stirring. Remove from heat and cool, stirring occasionally. Mix egg yolks and sugar together and beat until a light ribbon is formed. The mixture will be thick and creamy. Combine egg-sugar together with the milk-honey, whisking just to mix. Using a heavy-bottomed saucepan, return to medium-high heat and stir constantly until the mixture thickens. Remove immediately from the heat and pour through a fine strainer into a large bowl and cool, stirring occasionally. Add heavy cream and mix well. Chill mixture thoroughly. Make ice cream according to your ice cream machine's instructions. Serve garnished with crystalized violets.

Tautog with Asparagus and Vegetables
Your Favorite Salad
Fried Bread
Fresh Fruit
Cheeses

Serves four

In recent years, there seems to be a tendency in folks to not automatically eat dessert. Perhaps this is because we've all become more concerned about calories and sugar intake in general, but maybe we never really craved sugar that much anyway. Maybe cooks just kept thrusting desserts on us automatically because desserts are fun to cook and supposedly complete a meal. Cintra and I have tried to stay away from heavy desserts in this book because they do not compliment fish and seem actually to contradict the idea of a light, low-calorie main course. Fruit is a perfect dessert if you truly must have a sweet after fish. See the "Basics" chapter or index for suggestions on salads if you don't have your own favorite. The recipe for Fried Bread can be found on page 110.

TAUTOG WITH ASPARAGUS AND VEGETABLES

    2 lbs. tautog fillets
    1 leek, white part only, cut into 2"
        by ¼" julienne
    2 medium carrots, cut into a 2" by
        ¼" julienne
    1 celery stalk, cut into 2" by ¼"
        julienne
    1 lb. asparagus, cut into 2" pieces,
        peeled, blanched, refreshed in
        ice water and drained
    2 Idaho potatoes, cooked, peeled
        and quartered
    1 tomato, peeled, seeded and
        coarsely chopped and set aside
    1 tbsp. chopped chives
 1½ cups heavy cream
    2 tbsp. unsalted butter
      Salt and pepper
  ½ cup fish stock, or mild chicken
        stock, or if neither then just
        plain water

In heavy-bottomed cooking pot, sauté carrots, celery, and leek for 3 minutes in ½ tablespoon hot butter. Add ½ cup hot stock or water and a pinch of salt. Stir, cover for a few minutes and then remove cover to let most of the liquid evaporate. Any liquid left when the vegetables are cooked but crisp, add to the cream. Set vegetables aside. Pour cream into cooking casserole. Add the fish, a little salt and pepper and bring to a low simmer. Cook uncovered for 2 minutes and then drain off the cream. Add the carrots, leeks, celery, and asparagus to the fish. Add one potato to the cream. Put potato and cream in a food processor and blend only briefly (so as not to whip the cream). Add the rest of the potatoes. Blend again. Add 1 table-spoon plus 1 teaspoon butter, and season with salt and pepper. Pour this over fish and vegetables. Bring to a full boil. Remove from heat. Add chives and tomatoes and serve in heated soup plates with Fried Bread.

Stir-fried Snow Peas with Broccoli
Black Sea Bass Chinese Style
White Rice
Fortune Cookies

Serves four

I thought you would know how to cook white rice so I did not include a recipe for it. Also, I have found that rice lovers all have their own very definite ideas as to what brand, converted or not, sticky or dry the rice should be. Fortune cookies need to be bought.

STIR-FRY SNOW PEAS WITH BROCCOLI

1 head of broccoli
1 lb. snow peas, ends and strings
   removed
2 tbsp. sesame oil
2 tbsp. unsalted butter
Salt and pepper

Remove bite-size flowerettes from the broccoli and blanch. Heat the oil and butter together and add the snow peas and flowerettes. Stir constantly and till hot and season with salt and pepper.

BLACK SEA BASS CHINESE STYLE

    3 lbs. of black sea bass, the
        average size is 1-3 lbs, so 2
        smaller or 1 bigger
    2 tbsp. dry sherry
    3 tbsp. corn oil
    2 tbsp. sesame oil
    The juices from the cooked fish
    ¼ cup plus 2 tsp. soy sauce
    1 tsp. sugar
    3 tsp. cornstarch, mixed in ¼ cup
        cold water per cup liquid
    Salt and pepper
    5 scallions, white and green parts
        cleaned, in 1″ pieces
    4 tbsp. peeled and julienned
        ginger
    1 clove garlic, chopped fine
    ½ cup water

Bone, clean, wash and dry the fish and leave head and tail on. Score the fish on both sides and lay it on a large piece of foil. Combine the sherry and 2 teaspoons of soy sauce to make a basting liquid. Sprinkle the fish with the liquid and a grind of pepper and fold up carefully to encase all liquid. Steam over boiling water in steamer for 15 minutes. Meanwhile, in heavy saucepan, heat the two oils until hot. Lower heat and add ginger. Cook 1-2 minutes. Add scallions, garlic and cook 20 seconds. Add soy sauce, ½ cup water, sugar. Stir well and set aside. Remove fish from foil as soon as cooked. Save juices. If a lot, reduce to 5-6 tablespoons. Add to sauce. Season with salt and pepper. Pour over fish. Serve on a decorative platter.

———————————

Shellfish

I n a fish cookbook that is written for fishermen, why include a chapter about shellfish? Don't you know shellfish aren't fish and can't sportingly be caught with rod and line, dummy? The reason has to do with philosophy.

Knowles is a great fisherman. Ted has written about him several times now in *Gray's Sporting Journal* and he truly is becoming a legend in his own time. This is partially because he is such a humorous character and because he is old and has seen a lot and because we believe in making old people legends. But we all know, particularly in the hunting and fishing part of our lives, good and interesting characters. Knowles does go beyond that. Years ago now we used to go to Nantucket for the fish-all-night, sleep-all-day festival for striped bass. They were long, hard nights trudging around in heavy waders, casting waist-high in the surf, travelling up and down the long beaches in four-wheel drives looking for the ever-dwindling populace of striped bass. There were gamuts of emotion, beautiful sunrises, visions of Jaws lurking in inky-black waters, cold winds and jovial jeep-side conversation, all to end with daybreak and falling exhausted into bed. Except for Knowles who went to play golf. He'd been there on the beaches in his Willys catching more fish than anyone else, but for some reason he wasn't ever tired the next day. I kept imagining him as a three-year-old: his mother must have considered suicide versus trying to keep up with him. Even when Knowles couldn't find someone to play golf with, he didn't sleep, he just went somewhere.

I'd fished with Knowles, I'd drunk whisky with Knowles, it was time to travel with Knowles through the day that had a sleepless night. He drove me all over the island in his Willys, not to the town of Nantucket or to Siasconset or to the places the tourists saw or to places I'd ever seen before. Just to the places that were beautiful. And he knew the name of every tree, every bird, every flower that we saw. He stopped at last in front of a saltwater pond; you could see the ocean on the other side of the dune. There was a mound of shells, all one kind, all white, as high as I was. Beautiful scallop shells and he stared at them in wonderment. For just as Knowles will watch the birds to figure where to fish, he will find the hills of shells to find the scallop beds. Watching and concentrating on nature is it.

The contentedness derived from fishing is similar to that derived from collecting mussels or trapping lobsters. We observe and learn about nature in order to gather selectively from it, and to eat what is best from it. It is the same philosophy whether it's a fisherman's or a scalloper's.

**Oyster Stew
Grits
Your Own Nice Green Salad
Apple Tart**

Serves four

In my mind, for many years, I likened grits to oatmeal. They were gloppy and ugly and eaten not because they tasted good but because you wanted to stay warm or get warm or add bulk to your meal. This is still true in my mind about oatmeal but the image has completely changed concerning grits. Grits are absolutely delicious and Northerners should make more of an effort to incorporate them into their menus. There is still one similarity between grits and oatmeal. It's a good idea to add a lot of flavoring to the grits, like butter or cheese or cayenne. We also think it's a good idea to stay away from the quick cooking or instant grits. They're simply not as tasty.

OYSTER STEW

1-2 tbsp. unsalted butter
1 pint oysters
2 large shallots
  Salt and pepper
  Tiny pinch tarragon
3 cups light cream or mixture of
    heavy cream and milk

Drain oysters in a strainer, catching all liquid. Chop shallots extremely fine and sauté them in butter till translucent but not a bit browned. Add oyster liquid and milk/cream to shallots, salt and pepper and a tiny pinch of tarragon and bring to simmer. Let it sit on a low heat for 5-10 minutes and then add the oysters. Heat through to your taste, 2-3 minutes and serve.

GRITS

¾ cup grits—not quick cooking
3 cups boiling chicken stock—at
  least use Knorr chicken cubes,
  not canned stuff, unless it's
  College Inn
2 tsp. salt
  Pepper to taste
  A sprinkle of cayenne pepper
3 tbsp. unsalted butter
½ lb. grated gruyére cheese
2 eggs

Add grits to stock. Stir over medium-high heat until it bubbles and thickens, about 10-15 minutes. Remove from heat. Stir to cool slightly. Add eggs one at a time stirring after each. Season with salt and pepper and cayenne. Now add the cheese. Taste again and add any seasoning. Put in buttered gratin dish with 1 tablespoon of the butter. Dot with remaining butter. Bake for 1 hour. Let sit for a few minutes before serving.

APPLE TART

1 recipe for short pastry, or frozen
  pastry
5 McIntosh apples
2-3 tbsp. unsalted butter
  Cinnamon and sugar
1 cup heavy cream
1 tbsp. confectioners' sugar
1 tbsp. Calvados

Preheat oven to 425°. Roll pastry thin and rectangular in shape. Place on buttered aluminum cookie sheet. Let rest 1 hour in the refrigerator. Peel, core and slice apples thin. Arrange overlapping in any design on pastry. Sprinkle liberally with cinnamon and sugar and dot with butter. Bake till edges of pastry are nicely light brown. Slide onto cooling rack. Check bottom of pastry to see if it's sufficiently browned. Serve hot or cold, with whipped cream with a little confectioners' sugar and some Calvados in it.

Mussels Steamed
Grilled Lamb Chops
Caesar Salad
Fresh Fruit

Serves four

The recipe for Caesar salad can be used here as well. And you can choose where and how to grill the lamb chops.

MUSSELS STEAMED

4 qts. mussels (1 qt. per person)
2 cups white wine (or enough to
    cover the bottom of your pot
    by ½")
3 tbsp. shallots, finely chopped
1 tbsp. unsalted butter
2 cups heavy cream
3 egg yolks
  Salt and pepper
  Chopped parsley

Bring the wine to a boil. Place the mussels over the wine, not in it, and steam for about 10 or 15 minutes, or until they just pop open. You may need to stir the top mussels down to the bottom so all have an equal opportunity to open. Remove the mussels and pour the wine broth into a large bowl so the sand can settle to the bottom. Sauté the shallots in the butter and then carefully ladle the wine broth into the pan with the shallots. Reduce for a minute or two over a high heat. Meanwhile, in a small bowl beat the egg yolks together with the cream. Now beat in a few tablespoons of the broth. Add the entire egg yolk/cream mixture to the broth and whisk until mixed. Heat till slightly thickened and remove from heat. Add salt and pepper to taste. To serve, divide the mussels into four warmed soup plates and pour the egg broth over. Sprinkle with parsley and serve immediately.

Shrimp Gratin
Simple Green Salad

Serves four

Armagnac is a lesser grade of cognac and is usually cheaper than Courvoisier. I recommend it because you can really splash it on without seeing the dollar signs dribbled all over your shrimp.

SHRIMP GRATIN

32 medium cooked shrimp or
     whatever quantity you want
     for 4 people, or use 8 lobster
     tails
5 tbsp. unsalted butter, plus some
     for dotting
2 tbsp. flour
¼ cup dry white wine
1 tsp. tarragon
1 cup heavy cream reduced with
     the tarragon to ¾ cup
⅓ cup grated gruyére cheese
1 tbsp. mustard
     Salt and pepper and cayenne
     pepper
1 dash of Armagnac
½ cup breadcrumbs

Preheat oven to 325°. Make a light white sauce by combining first the butter, flour and white wine. Then add to it the reduced cream and tarragon, cheese, mustard, salt, peppers and Armagnac. Pour over the shrimp. Sprinkle with ½ cup breadcrumbs. Dot with 2 tablespoons butter and cook about 10-15 minutes until hot. Put under broiler until it bubbles, and serve.

Caesar Salad
Mussel Pizza

Serves four

One of the nice aspects of pizza is its versatility. It can be for lunch or dinner or hors d'oeuvres. It can be for children or grown-ups, it can be chic or casual, all depending on what you do with the toppings and what you serve with it. The intention for this menu is that it be used for a Sunday night supper with guests. (You can make just one of the pizzas with mussels and use the rest of the dough for a cheese and tomato sauce pizza for the kids.)

CAESAR SALAD

    2 heads Romaine lettuce, washed
         and dried
    1 garlic clove
    ½ cup good quality olive oil
    1 cup cubed French or Italian
         bread
    4 anchovy fillets, chopped very
         small
 1½ tsp. salt
 4-5 grinds of fresh pepper
    ¼ tsp. dry mustard
    ¼ tsp. Worcestershire sauce
    3 tbsp. red wine vinegar
    1 raw egg, lightly beaten
         Juice of 1 lemon, strained
    3 tbsp. Parmesan cheese

The night before, heat the garlic clove in the olive oil for 15 minutes. Remove from the heat and let sit overnight, and then discard the garlic. Sauté the cubes of bread in 2 tablespoons of the oil and set aside on a plate. Combine the remaining oil, lettuce and all the rest of the ingredients tossing very well. Now add the garlic croutons and toss again. Serve at once.

MUSSEL PIZZA

For the dough:

2⅔ cups unbleached all-purpose
    flour
⅓ cup whole wheat flour
1 pkg. yeast
1⅓ cups warm water
1 tsp. salt
2 tsp. dried thyme

Dissolve the yeast in 1⅓ cups warm water. Reconstitute the thyme in a bit of hot water. In a large bowl, combine the thyme with both flours and salt. Stir the yeast/water with a fork and pour into a "well" you've made in the center of the flour mixture. With your fork, gradually bring flour into the "well" until the yeast/water is fairly well combined with the flour mixture. Form into a ball and turn out onto a floured surface. Knead for five minutes. Put the dough in a bowl rubbed with olive oil and cover with a clean towel. Place the bowl in a warm spot and let the dough rise till it's doubled (about 1½ hours).

For the pizza topping:

2 qts. mussels, cleaned and de-
    bearded
2 cups white wine
1 garlic clove, mashed
  A few parsley stems
  A couple of peppercorns
  Olive oil
  Lemon juice
2 cups shredded mozzarella cheese
½ cup finely chopped parsley

Combine the white wine, parsley stems, garlic, and peppercorns in a large pot. Steam the mussels over the white wine, not in it, till they just start to open and remove immediately. Spread around in one layer on the counter to cool fast. Open and remove mussels to a large bowl and toss with olive oil and lemon juice. (You can also open mussels by placing them in a microwave for a few seconds.) Preheat the oven to 450°. Divide the dough in half and roll out into two 12″ circles. Place on a cookie sheet or pizza stone. Layer the mozzarella on and then add the mussels and sprinkle with parsley, red pepper flakes and olive oil. Bake for 15 minutes or until the edges are crispy.

Egg and Asparagus Salad
Little Shrimp
Baked Apples

Serves four

I believe the next stage in the growth and development of our cooking and eating tastes in the United States will be more emphasis on regional foods. We've all been through the fads of French, Northern Italian and Chinese cooking and incorporated into our own style the best of those cuisines. But we are moving now to understanding and appreciating what is locally fresh and uniquely different from the rest of the country or world. This involves not just appreciating the style of Cajun cooking or Southern food, but truly understanding that New Jersey blueberries are different from those grown in Maine or Michigan. One can barely use some of Alice Waters' cookbooks if living outside of California.

To discover your own local treats and invent the cooking methods for them has got to be one of the great delights in cooking. It is also a very good reason to fish. I use this recipe for shrimp on one of our local species which the fishermen call scampi and is available only in the Spring. These shrimp are divine. I hope you will find the recipe useful on your shrimp or when you come to New England in the Spring.

EGG AND ASPARAGUS SALAD

2 hard-boiled eggs	1 tsp. prepared mustard
½ lb. asparagus, peeled	½ cup olive oil
2 heads Boston lettuce, cleaned and dried	1 tbsp. mayonnaise
1 tbsp. vinegar	Salt and pepper

To hard-boil the eggs, set in cold water with a tablespoon of white vinegar, bring to a boil, reduce to a medium simmer and cook, using a timer, for 9 minutes. Then plunge in cold water. Peel, chop and set aside.

Steam the asparagus, cut into 1″ pieces and combine with the lettuce. Make a vinaigrette by combining in the blender the vinegar, mustard, oil and dashes of salt and pepper and blending for a second or two. Add the mayonnaise and motorize for another second. Toss the vinaigrette first with the asparagus and lettuce and then add chopped egg. Toss lightly, taste for salt and pepper and serve.

LITTLE SHRIMP

2½ lbs. tiny shrimp
4 tbsp. unsalted butter
2 tbsp. Armagnac
1 cup heavy cream
  Salt and freshly ground pepper

The tiny shrimp from Maine or the little San Francisco Bay shrimp are superb. You cook them whole, heads and tails and the shell and eat at the table. It's very messy but worth it at least once a year.

Clean the shrimp of debris. They often come with star fish, etc. Try not to wash unless they are gritty. In a large frying pan over medium high heat cook butter stirring until it is a light brown color. Add shrimp instantly and cook on high heat shaking or stirring until shells turn red. Remove from heat and cover pan for about 5 minutes. This will finish the cooking. With a slotted spoon scoop out shrimp to a platter. Return pan to high heat and add Armagnac. Let bubble a little and then add cream and cook until reduced by half. Taste for seasoning and add salt and pepper as necessary. Add shrimp and oozed out liquid to the pan and reheat. Taste for seasoning again and serve immediately with French bread to mop up the sauce. Remove the head, pull off the shell and what a delicious treat!

BAKED APPLES

4 large apples, cored and with
    their tops cut off
4 tbsp. marmalade
4 tsp. raisins
1 stick unsalted butter
1 store-bought yellow (pound or
    genoise) cake
1½ cups heavy cream
1 tbsp. confectioners' sugar
1½ tbsp. Grand Marnier liqueur

Stuff the opening in each apple with marmalade and raisins. Dot with butter and bake at 325° for approximately 40 minutes. While the apples are cooking, fry 4 ⅜" slices of yellow cake in about 4 tablespoons unsalted butter. Combine and whip lightly the cream, sugar and Grand Marnier. To serve, set each apple on a slice of cake. Pour cooking juices around and pass on the side the lightly whipped cream.

Lobster with Anchovy Garlic Butter
Tomato Bread
Your Simplest Green Salad
Drunk Melons

Serves four

Your salad is good here or refer to the index or "Basics" chapter in this book for suggestions.

LOBSTER WITH ANCHOVY BUTTER

4 1-lb. lobsters
1 cup good olive oil
8 peeled garlic cloves
1½ tsp. thyme
1 bay leaf

Kill the lobsters in boiling water if you must, but it is easier to do so by inserting a sharp knife just where the head joins the shell to cut the spinal cord. Turn the lobster over and cut carefully through the cartilage, down the length of the body. Open it out, (save coral and tamale) and crack the claws. Heat on low heat the oil, garlic, thyme, and bay leaf for 20-30 minutes. Remove garlic and bay leaf and keep the garlic for whatever sounds good. Brush the lobsters with the oil and grill flesh side down 7 minutes. Turn and put a dollop of the anchovy garlic butter on and cook for another 2 minutes. The lobsters are cooked when the flesh is just opaque.

ANCHOVY GARLIC BUTTER

1½ sticks unsalted butter
1 large or 2 medium cloves
   garlic—mashed with the side
   of a knife and then chopped
   very fine
1 anchovy fillet, chopped fine
   Salt and pepper and a squeeze
   of lemon juice

Make in advance. Whip the butter until fluffy. Add the remaining ingredients and whip again. Place onto plastic wrap and mold into a log shape. Freeze for at least 24 hours and then bring into the refrigerator about an hour before it is to be used.

TOMATO BREAD

8 ½-inch slices French or Italian
    bread or a good country whole
    wheat
4 ripe good (they must be very
    good) tomatoes, peeled,
    seeded and coarsely chopped
1 pinch basil
    Salt and pepper
    Approximately ½ cup olive oil

On cookie sheet bake the bread at 300° until just light golden.
Cook the tomatoes in 1 tablespoon olive oil over medium heat until most of the liquid has evaporated and they start to mush together. Cool. Spread a very small amount over each slice of bread and drizzle with olive oil. Sprinkle with salt and pepper and serve at once.

DRUNK MELONS

2 very ripe melons (They may be
    2 different varieties.)
½ cup champagne brandy
½ cup Curacao
    Sprinkle of confectioners' sugar
    Mint leaves

Remove a lid off the most attractive of the melons. Take out all seeds and scoop out the melon in small pieces. Cut the second melon in half and dice in large pieces or scoop. Put all melon pieces in a bowl. Sprinkle with the confectioners' sugar, champagne brandy and curacao. Stir and let sit for about an hour. To serve, put back in the melon shell, top with mint and cover with lid.

Crab Cakes with Sherry and Garlic Mayonnaise
Chicory Salad

Serves four

CRAB CAKES WITH SHERRY AND GARLIC MAYONNAISE

   1 cup very finely minced celery
   1 cup very finely minced onion
8-10 tbsp. unsalted butter
   2 lbs. fresh crabmeat—cleaned of
        all cartilage
   2 tbsp. Worcestershire sauce
1½ tsp. Tabasco sauce
      Juice of 1 lemon
      Salt and pepper
   3 tbsp. very finely chopped parsley
   3 egg yolks
   1 whole egg
   ¼ cup heavy cream
   3 tsp. dry mustard
   4 cups fresh bread crumbs (see
        page 210)
2½ cups flour
   ¾ cup milk

Cook onion and celery in the 4 tablespoons butter until translucent and wilted but not browned. Add to the crabmeat the Worcestershire sauce, Tabasco sauce, lemon juice, salt and pepper, parsley, and 3 tablespoons breadcrumbs. Mix together the egg yolks, heavy cream and dry mustard and combine with the crabmeat. Refrigerate for 1 hour or until thoroughly cooled. Then gently shape into patties.

Beat the whole egg and milk together. Dip the patties into flour, then using a pastry brush, paint with egg/milk mixture and then dip into bread crumbs. Do this gently, covering all surfaces. Place on a cooling rack and let rest in refrigerator for 30 minutes to 1 hour. To cook, heat 4 to 6 tablespoons of butter to sizzling and brown each crab cake about 4 minutes first side and 2½ to 3 on the second side. Serve with the sherry and garlic mayonnaise.

SHERRY AND GARLIC MAYONNAISE

        3 egg yolks
        ⅓ cup sherry vinegar
        2 tsp. prepared mustard
        ½ tsp. salt
        ¼ tsp. ground pepper
        8 garlic cloves, blanched, peeled
              and chopped finely
           Several dashes of cayenne
        2 cups oil—corn or good olive

In a bowl combine: sherry vinegar, garlic, salt, mustard, pepper, cayenne. Let salt melt. Add egg yolks. Whisk until frothy and well combined. Add oil very slowly in a dribble until the mayonnaise seems to have started to thicken, then you may add the oil faster. When finished, taste for seasoning and adjust with salt, pepper, mustard, or sherry vinegar. Be sure to dissolve the salt in the sherry vinegar first as it will not dissolve as well in the mayonnaise. Whisk in a tablespoon of hot, hot water to finish it. This may be done in the food processor with no fuss/no mess.

CHICORY SALAD

        1 small head chicory
        1 head Boston lettuce
        1 small bunch watercress
        6 slices medium crisp bacon, or
              better yet, pancetta

For the dressing:

        3 tbsp. vinegar
           Salt and pepper
        1 tsp. prepared mustard
        1 tsp. tarragon, revived in a little
              hot water
        1 very small clove garlic, mashed
              and then chopped very fine
        ¼ cup olive oil

Wash the greens carefully. Shake dry and roll up in clean terry towels. (This can be done several hours before using.) Combine all the ingredients for the dressing in a blender and blend on high. Toss salad with dressing. Add bacon or pancetta and then taste and adjust seasoning.

Szechwan Crab for Sunday Night Supper
White Rice with Soy Sauce on the Side
Stir Fried Pea Pods

Serves four

The white rice should be cooked the way you like it (I'm an unconverted rice fan, although I was brought up on Uncle Ben's and still have not had the courage to tell my mother that I don't use it). Some very unusual and interesting soy sauces are now available in regular grocery stores and are worth experimenting with to find what you like. Chinese grocery stores and gourmet shops still offer a good selection, too.

The pea pods in this menu just need the tips cut and strings pulled off. Then sauté quickly in unsalted butter until hot. Season with salt and pepper.

SZECHWAN CRAB FOR SUNDAY NIGHT SUPPER

1¼ lbs. fresh crab cut into 2″ pieces
5 tbsp. peanut oil
6 scallions, chopped into ¹⁄₁₆″ pieces—white part and ⅓ of the green
2 tbsp. ginger, peeled and chopped fine (1″ of whole ginger = 1 tbsp. chopped ginger)
1 tbsp. Chinese rice wine
1 tsp. salt
4 eggs
½ tsp. sugar

Mix together the crabmeat, scallions, all but ½ tbsp. of the ginger, rice wine, and salt. Let sit for 20 minutes. Beat the eggs together and set aside.

Heat pan over medium high heat. Add oil. Just as it starts to bubble, add drained crabmeat/scallion mixture, plus the rest of the ginger and the sugar. Stir well for 1-2 minutes. Now add the wine and liquid drained from the crabmeat mixture. Taste for seasoning. You may need up to ½ tsp. of additional salt (don't worry if it seems like a lot). Fry another minute or so. Then add eggs, stirring constantly for another minute or two, until the eggs are thoroughly cooked. Serve immediately.

Freshwater Fish

I had a rather eclectic relationship with fish as a child. As a tiny little girl I have very far away memories of the commercial fishing boats on Lake Michigan, walking the beaches looking for the metal floats washed up from their nets, and my parents eating delicious "whitefish" for breakfast. But by the time I'd become old enough to catch the fish, the Great Lakes had become barren of edible fish and my greatest source and opportunity for catching and eating fish was gone. My parents resorted to eating fish that had been "brought in." The fish stores liked to claim that the fish had been flown in, but we could tell from the aroma and taste of the fish that it had actually travelled by wagon train and come down the Erie Canal. Fresh they were not. There were many years which passed where I stood firm on the belief that fish was not very tasty. In bits and pieces I began to learn something about fishing on my annual trips to Florida, but fishing and eating fish remained separate concepts for me for a long time.

The idea that the best fish to eat is the fish you've caught, and vice versa, came to me in two quick, hard lessons. As a teenager cruising on a sailboat in the North Channel, I discovered something I'd never done before: fishing in Lake Superior. Still rather barren of fish and me completely unknowledgeable about freshwater fishing, I was reduced to the little rock bass which lay along the pier where we were moored. The minnows netted proved excellent bait and I caught literally 50 or 60 little rock bass. Catch-and-release was not a known concept to me, especially for rock bass, and the little fish lay scattered on the dock. A passing gentleman, seeing the litter of dead fish exclaimed, "I hope you intend to eat every one of those." It was as if an enormous tidal wave of realization came over me: *Most people eat what they catch!* And as I looked at all those dead fish I understood what a dreadful thing I had done. Only the excuse of providing sustenance could have absolved me.

Clearly there was no brain in this pathetic fisherman but I was at least now armed with a new conscience (and primed for the concept of catch-and-release). I did have the good sense to travel East and marry a fisherman. Although at this point I realized that morally it was tasteless to not eat what you caught and kept, I still was a little slow to understand the selfish benefits to it all. Ed and I were invited up to Maine to a friend's lovely old log cabin for fishing. We had the place to ourselves. The seven hour car ride had been long, especially the last hour on dirt roads. We felt particularly welcomed as we drove up to the house and saw the caretaker waiting for us with a little stringer of native brook trout. He had just finished building a fire and was breaking off sticks to skewer the fish as we were unloading the car. We sat by the water eating the roasted brook trout. I had had brook trout in restaurants in the Midwest before; were these fish related? Impossible. As that wave of conscience had washed over me, so now did a new wave of eating delight. A freshly caught, wild fish, simply cooked; this surely was the ultimate taste treat. From there to catching the fish myself and eating it fresh, the lesson was forever locked in my mind, heart and taste buds.

I have never tasted a fresh fish that I didn't like. Much of this cookbook is concerned with cooking and eating very fresh fish and is written on the premise that a good, fresh fish need not have much done to it. The fresher the fish, the simpler the recipe for its preparation. Do not let yourself get enticed for the sake of culinary art into cooking sauces and court boullions and complicated programs for a fresh fish. There's no need to over-cook. Save all that for the rest of the menu or an old fish. Relax, and think of fresh fish as your chance to cook the simplest, but most delicious food there is.

I have in many of the menus here tried very hard to keep the fish recipes simple because that is what makes the fish taste best. Sometimes I have made the rest of the menu more complicated to keep up your interest in cooking, but on other occasions I've complimented the simplicity of the fish recipe with a simple menu: Pumpkinseed-Fish-On-A-Stick with Homemade Chocolate Chip Cookies. If only that had been my first meal of a fish I'd caught, it never would have taken me twenty-five years to love to fish and eat the fish I catch.

The Stream Fish

I think God really wanted us to eat the fish we catch, but He realized there were a bunch of pigs in the crowd and so He invented the sport fisherman: A creature who would find it appealing just to catch the fish and would figure out a whole lot of excuses why we all should put the fish back and not eat it. The fishermen have used both guilt, as in the case of the striped bass (our chemical effluents have been killing the fry in the Chesapeake), and reason very effectively to make us put it all back.

When we go fishing in Alaska for rainbow trout, the guides are very proud of the fact that they may have had to kill only one trout, or maybe none at all, that summer. They are very protective of those trout and tell the fisherman that they aren't worth catching to eat anyway because they don't taste very good. A trout that doesn't taste good, is this possible? Oh, yes, it's because the rainbows feed on carcasses of the dead salmon. They must taste terrible feeding on that stuff. If this logic followed we would want to reduce our fish intake considerably. Note the lovely aroma and appeal of your chum bucket some time; and doesn't that sea worm look scrumptious? Unlike the duck that feeds on wild rice or the antelope that grazes on sage-scented grasses, fish are not known for their gourmet diets. It probably is a little difficult to honestly say that carcass-eating rainbows taste any worse than the ones that eat lemmings or salmon eggs or insects.

There is perhaps more correlation between where the fish lives and his flavor than to how his diet affects his taste. It does seem that the little brookies, the Dolly Varden, grayling or rainbow trout that swim in the beautiful wild waters of Alaska, British Columbia, or Montana or Maine are better eating than hatchery trout.

Or is it simply that we like to catch the fish in those places? God did intend for us to eat the fish we catch.

Breakfast Trout
Cornbread

Serves four

BREAKFAST TROUT

4 ⅛″ slices of pancetta (Italian cured bacon)
4 12-oz. trout, cleaned, whole
1 cup flour
   Salt and fresh ground pepper
   Lemon wedges
½ cup clarified butter
1 tbsp. plus 2 tsp. pancetta fat
20 cherry tomatoes

Slice the pancetta into ½″ strips and sauté on low heat until almost crisp. Set on towels to drain. Rinse trout, drain; sprinkle with salt and pepper. Dredge in flour; shake off excess. Fry in hot butter and 1 tablespoon pancetta fat 3-4 minutes per side. Set on warm plates when done and sauté cherry tomatoes in same pan, adding 2 teaspoons pancetta fat to the pan. Reheat the pancetta strips with the tomatoes. Divide among the plates and garnish with lemon wedges.

CORNBREAD

1½ cups cornmeal
2 tsp. baking powder
1 tsp. salt
¼ cup flour
2 tbsp. sugar
2 eggs
1 cup buttermilk
3 tbsp. bacon drippings

Sift together the cornmeal, baking powder, salt, sugar, and flour. Beat the eggs, then add the buttermilk and bacon drippings and combine with the dry ingredients. Bake in a 425° oven for 15 to 25 minutes (depending on whether you cook in a square pan, cornstick molds or muffin tins).

Trout Fried
Stuffed Risotto Tomatoes
Zucchini
Strawberry Sponge

Serves four

TROUT FRIED

2 trout, boned and filleted
2 tbsp. flour
1 egg
1 tsp. oil
1 tsp. water
¼ tsp. thyme
4 tbsp. unsalted butter
4 slices of French bread or a
     generous ½ cup of bread
     crumbs
  Salt and pepper

Process four slices of dry French bread in your food processor and sift through a wire mesh strainer. Put the flour on a plate and dust both sides of the fish. Combine the egg, oil, water and thyme and using a pastry brush, paint the fillets with this mixture. Now dip the trout into breadcrumbs and rest on a cake rack to dry. This can be done ½ hour before cooking. (If you leave the skin on put flour only on the skin side. Use the egg mixture and crumbs for the flesh side only.) Heat the butter in a large skillet until very hot. Put in fish and cook only a few minutes on each side. It will be very crispy on the outside and moist on the inside. The fish may be kept warm for a few minutes. Serve with lemon wedges.

STUFFED RISOTTO TOMATOES

4 medium-sized tomatoes, ripe but
   firm
2 tbsp. tomato purée
2 tbsp. Parmesan cheese
   Sprinkle of bread crumbs
   Dots of butter
   Salt and pepper
   Dribble of oil

Remove tops and carefully scoop out seeds. Sprinkle with salt and pepper. Dot with oil and bake at 425° for 5-6 minutes. Remove from oven, drain juices and save. Make risotto according to the directions on page 209. Stir in the purée, Parmesan cheese, and the juices you reserved from the tomatoes. This can be done several hours ahead. Sprinkle with fresh bread crumbs. Dot with butter and bake at 425° for 10-15 minutes.

ZUCCHINI

8 5″ to 6″ firm zucchini
1 small clove garlic, chopped fine
   (optional)
2-3 tbsp. unsalted butter
   Salt and pepper

Cut both ends off the zucchinis. Cut in half lengthwise and then in half again so that each zucchini is in 4 long pieces. Cut each piece into ⅛″ thick strips and then cut the strips in half. You now have zucchini that looks like pasta. Melt butter. When very hot, add zucchini and garlic. Cook over medium high heat until soft. Season with salt and pepper and serve.

STRAWBERRY SPONGE

1 supermarket sponge cake
4 egg yolks
1 cup heavy cream
⅓ cup sugar
¼ tsp. salt
1 tsp. vanilla extract
3 tbsp. framboise or Grand
    Marnier, or rum
Several tbsp. melted currant
    jelly

Paint the sponge cake with a tablespoon or so of the framboise if you have it or Grand Marnier or even rum will do. Mix the egg yolks and sugar in a bowl with a whisk. Add salt and cream. Mix well but do not whisk to a foam. Transfer to a heavy bottomed sauce pan. Put over high or medium high heat and stir constantly with a wooden spoon (that means touching the bottom of the pan as you stir) until the custard begins to thicken and the surface of the custard becomes very smooth. Pour immediately through a strainer into another bowl and whisk to cool to stop the cooking. Then add two tablespoons of the liqueur and the vanilla and chill for several hours stirring occasionally. Spread the custard on the cake base and top with straw-berries and glaze with the melted currant jelly. If not served at once, it may be chilled for a bit. Just bring it out of the refrigerator 15 minutes or so before eating.

Poached Steelhead Trout with Lemon Butter Sauce
Fava Beans with Asparagus
Strawberries and Crème Anglais

Serves four

Fava beans are hard to find, especially anywhere outside of California, but worth a hard search. Skip the canned version.

POACHED STEELHEAD TROUT WITH LEMON BUTTER SAUCE

4 steaks, ¾–1″ thick. One steak
    per person should do,
    depending on the size of the
    fish.
½ cup plus 2 tbsp. vinegar
1½ quarts water
1 tbsp. salt
2 peppercorns, crushed
    Pinch thyme
½ bay leaf
1 onion, thinly sliced
1 carrot, sliced
2 shallots, chopped fine and
    sautéed in butter
¼ cup white wine
8 oz. plus a tbsp. unsalted butter
    Salt and pepper

Make a court bouillon by combining ½ cup vinegar, water, 1 tablespoon salt, peppercorns, bay leaf, onion and carrot and bringing to a boil. Cook 45 minutes. Strain and let cool.

Now combine together the 2 tablespoons of vinegar, wine, salt and pepper and cooked shallots and reduce by ½ to ⅔. Set aside.

Return the court bouillon to the stove and bring to a boil. Plunge the fish steaks in. Bring back to boil. Cover and remove from the heat. The steaks should take 7-8 minutes. Drain the fish and place on warm plates.

Return the vinegar wine reduction to heat and at a hot but not boiling temperature, add the butter in small bits, whisking constantly. The sauce will become foamy and white. Serve immediately on the fish.

FAVA BEANS WITH ASPARAGUS

3-4 lbs. fava beans
1 lb. asparagus
2 tbsp. unsalted butter
Salt and pepper

Fava beans are a wonderful spring vegetable. Big supermarkets will probably carry them as well as Italian markets. A lot of tedious work is involved in preparing them, so you may only eat them once a year, but it's worth it for the taste and the fact that they mean spring is here. Remove fava beans from their pods. Peel the outer skin from each bean (it is worth it, I promise). Steam until just done—about 5 minutes. Refresh with ice water and drain. Remove the tips from the asparagus and use the stalks for soup. Blanch or steam the tips until just done. Refresh in ice water and drain. This can all be done in the morning. Cook the butter until sizzling (you could use ½ bacon fat if you wish). Add beans and asparagus. Cook until vegetables are heated through. Season with salt and pepper. Serve.

STRAWBERRIES WITH CRÈME ANGLAIS

1 pt. fresh strawberries, cleaned
   and hulled
½ cup milk
½ cup heavy cream
4 egg yolks
¼ cup sugar
⅛ tsp. salt
1 tbsp. liqueur or vanilla (Grand
   Marnier is good)

Whisk together the yolks, salt and sugar. Combine the milk and cream and whisk that together with the yolk combination. Cook over a medium-high heat stirring constantly until it thickens quite suddenly. Remove from the heat, strain and whisk cool. Add the liqueur or vanilla and spoon over the strawberries.

Trout with Noisette Butter
Sautéed Cucumbers
Dilled New Potatoes

Serves four

TROUT WITH NOISETTE BUTTER

4 trout
8 tbsp. unsalted butter
1 tbsp. corn oil
  Flour for dredging
  Salt and pepper
  Lemon juice

Clean the fish, removing intestines and gills. Wash and dry the fish and rub with oil and sprinkle with salt and pepper. Dredge in flour and shake off excess. Cook 4 tablespoons butter over medium heat until it is a very pale brown. Remove from heat and it will continue to cook a little more. If it appears to be turning color too fast, pour it into a cool pan to stop the cooking. Set this browned or noisette butter aside for the sauce. Heat 4 tablespoons of butter and all the oil together on medium-high until just about to sizzle. Add the trout and sauté until one side is golden and then turn and finish the other side. Remember, the second side will take a little less time. Serve the fish immediately, sprinkled first with lemon juice and then pour on the hot noisette butter.

SAUTÉED CUCUMBERS

4 cucumbers peeled, halved and
    seeded and cut into ¼″
    thick slices
2 tbsp. unsalted butter

Sauté in the hot butter until just tender. Season with salt and pepper.

DILLED NEW POTATOES

3 potatoes per person
1 tbsp. chopped dill
    Salt and pepper

Boil or steam the new potatoes and then sprinkle with the salt, pepper and dill.

Streamside Trout with Potatoes
Brownies

Serves four

For the best brownie recipe, see page 154.

STREAMSIDE TROUT WITH POTATOES

4 trout, cleaned and scaled
4 medium potatoes, cleaned and
   chopped with skin on, cut into
   bite size pieces
4 stalks celery, cleaned and
   chopped
4 ⅛"-thick slices of pancetta
   (Pancetta is a cured Italian
   Bacon. It is round in shape,
   carried by most delicatessans
   and may be eaten cooked, or
   uncooked. If you can't or
   don't wish to bring it on your
   fishing trip, then cook it at
   home and bring the rendered
   grease.)
Salt and pepper

Slice the pancetta into ½" strips and sauté till almost crisp. Spoon out a little of the fat into a cup (to cook the fish in), add the celery and potatoes to the rest. Cover and cook till nicely browned, turning once or twice. Season with salt and pepper. Push aside and add the extra fat and fish. Cook the fish until the tails are just crispy and season with salt and pepper.

**Grilled Char with Tarragon and Shallot Butter
Pasta with Fresh Corn and Basil
Sautéed Cherry Tomatoes
The Best Brownies**

Serves four

GRILLED CHAR WITH TARRAGON AND SHALLOT BUTTER

          4 char steaks
     1½ sticks unsalted butter
          1 tbsp. dried tarragon
     3-4 shallots finely chopped
          1 dash Worcestershire sauce
              Salt and pepper
              Oil for basting

Make the compound butter in advance. Whip the butter until light and fluffy. Add salt and pepper, Worcestershire, tarragon and shallots. Mix well and mound onto plastic wrap. Form into a cylinder and freeze for 24 hours. Bring to room temperature before using. Brush the char with oil and cook 6-8 minutes per side. Place pats of the compound butter on each steak and serve.

PASTA WITH FRESH CORN AND BASIL

          1 lb. pasta
     1½ cups cooked fresh corn
          1 cup heavy cream, reduced by ½
              Salt and pepper
          1 tsp. dried basil, cooked with the
                  cream
              Pinch cayenne pepper
              Lots of fresh basil for garnish

While the pasta is cooking, reduce the cream with the dried basil. Add cooked corn. Season with salt and pepper and cayenne and combine with the cooked pasta, check for seasoning again and serve.

SAUTÉED CHERRY TOMATOES

    24 cherry tomatoes
     2 tbsp. unsalted butter
        Several sprigs of dill (or any
           other herb you may have;
           dried herbs work, too)
        Salt and pepper

Prick each cherry tomato with a pin to prevent the tomato skins from bursting and remove the green tops. Sauté in the butter till hot and sprinkle with chopped herbs and salt and pepper. Serve.

THE BEST BROWNIES

     2 squares unsweetened chocolate
     1 stick unsalted butter
     1 cup sugar
     2 eggs
     1 tsp. vanilla
    ¼ cup flour
    ¼ tsp. salt
     1 cup chopped walnuts

Preheat oven to 325°. Melt together the chocolate and butter and then stir in the sugar. Beat together the eggs and vanilla and add them to the chocolate mixture. Now quickly stir in the flour, salt and chopped nuts. Spread in greased 8″×8″ pan and bake 40–45 minutes at 325°. Do not overcook or they will be dry. Cake tester should just come out clean. Let cool in pan. Then cut in squares and remove. The first brownie will be hard to get out and may stick and crumble. Do not be deterred. These are the best brownies.

Pan Poached Grayling
Sautéed Potatoes with Chanterelles and Thyme
Green Salad
Fresh Fruit with Lightly-whipped Cream
Almond Cookies

Serves four

When I think of eating grayling, I always think of a streamside meal. This would be a good menu streamside especially if you did the chopping of herbs and whatnot before leaving home and had them ready to go in a Baggie. Then lay the grayling fillets in foil, pour the wine over them and dump the prechopped herbs, parsley, celery, and shallots from their Baggie over the fish and seal the foil. Wrap again and cook in the coals of a wood fire. The potatoes and chanterelles can be done in a fry-pan over the coals, too. The fruit and cookies should be pre-prepared and ready to go. Just whip a little cream and you have a most elegant streamside dinner.

PAN POACHED GRAYLING

4 fillets
3-4 tbsp. unsalted butter
⅔ cup white wine
1 tsp. chopped parsley stems
1 small rib celery, peeled and
    diced
2 tsp. finely chopped shallots
  Salt and pepper
  Optional—any chopped fresh
    herbs, such as tarragon,
    parsley, chives

Sauté the shallots and celery with parsley stems in 1 tablespoon butter. Add the wine and simmer for a few minutes. Add the fish. Cover and reduce heat and cook until just tender. Remove the fish and reduce the liquid by ½ over high heat. Lower the heat and whisk in 2-3 tbsp. sweet butter. Season with salt and pepper. Stir in the herbs if you've chosen to use any. It is fine without. Pour over fish and serve.

SAUTÉED POTATOES WITH CHANTERELLES AND THYME

4 medium potatoes, peeled,
    washed and dried and cut into
    medium chunks
2 cups chanterelle mushrooms,
    coarsely chopped
5 tbsp. butter
1 tbsp. bacon fat
½ tsp. thyme
  Salt and pepper

If you are using dried mushrooms, rinse them quickly in cold water and revive them in a small amount of hot water or hot chicken stock. (You may save the liquid for another dish as it will permeate it with the flavor of the mushrooms.) In a large heavy-bottomed sauce pan melt bacon fat and 3 tablespoons of the butter until hot and sizzling. Add potatoes and sprinkle with salt and pepper. Cover and cook slowly. Let them brown slowly as they cook, stirring from time to time. At the same time, sauté the mushrooms in 2 tablespoons sweet butter for 1 minute over medium high heat. Lower the heat and sprinkle with salt and pepper and cover. Cook until juices exude, then remove cover, raise heat and evaporate juices stirring all the while. Add these to the cooked potatoes and sprinkle with thyme. Taste for seasoning and serve.

GREEN SALAD

1 head Boston, red, oakleaf lettuce
   or bibb (no strong tastes)
1 tbsp. vinegar
1 tsp. prepared mustard
½ cup oil
1 tsp. basil
   Salt and pepper

Blend all but the lettuce in the blender on high-speed. Toss with the lettuce.

For the fresh fruit, whip 1 cup cream lightly with a little liqueur or rum and 1 teaspoon confectioners' sugar.

ALMOND COOKIES

¾ cup unsalted butter, softened
½ cup sugar
¼ tsp. salt
1 egg
½ tbsp. orange rind
2 cups cake flour
   Dash of almond extract

Cream the butter into the sugar and salt. Whip till fluffy. Add 1 egg, orange rind and almond extract and mix. Blend in the flour. Cover the dough and refrigerate until it is firm. Roll out in small batches and cut with a cookie cutter. If you have it, use a fish cookie cutter to flatter the fishermen. Sprinkle with cinnamon sugar and bake at 350° till just starting to brown around the edges (about 7 minutes or so).

Leftover Char Risotto
Your Nice Green Salad
Tuscan Muffins
Apricot Crème Brulée

Serves four

Cintra and I have had our disagreements with this dessert about how long to cook the custard in the oven. I think we have disagreed partially because our ovens cook differently (hers is much hotter than mine) and partially because she is of the belief that custard should be quite soft. I like it any which way. Actually, I have determined after some experimentation that how long it cooks in the oven is somewhat dependent on how long you cook it on top of the stove. The 25 minutes specified here requires a short (3-5 minutes) amount of cooking on top of the stove. If you are willing to be quite diligent and stir the cream and egg mixture constantly until it is very hot, the cooking time in the oven should be reduced to 20 minutes or less, depending on how you like your custard.

LEFTOVER CHAR RISOTTO

        2 red peppers
        1 green pepper
        2 onions, chopped very fine
        4 oz. unsalted butter or a mixture
             of butter and olive oil
     1½ cups Italian arborio rice
     4-5 cups hot fluid, either stock or
             water or a combination of both
     1½ cups any leftover char, broken
             into pieces, fat and bones
             removed.
        2 tbsp. chopped Italian parsley

First, halve the peppers and take out the seeds (or use whole). Place them cut-side down on a piece of foil in the broiler and broil them 2 to 3 minutes until the skins are black. Remove and let cool. Peel the black skin off, remove the seeds and slice the peppers into pieces.

Then, in a heavy-bottomed, wide saucepan, heat butter. Sauté onions until translucent. Add rice. Cook, stirring until it becomes very white, shiny and very hot to touch. Then, over medium–high heat, add only enough stock so that the rice is just covered. Holding the handle of the saucepan, firmly swish the rice around and around. Do this every 2-3 minutes, keeping a low simmer going in the pot in between. This is so the rice won't stick. (If you weaken and stir the rice, then you must continue to stir until done.) As soon as you can distinguish the grains of rice again, then add another ½ cup of fluid. Keep swirling the pot and adding more fluid as it becomes absorbed. Taste when you feel it is nearly finished. It should be firm to the bite, and tender, creamy texture—not too dry and not too runny. In the meantime, sauté the peppers separately (red from green) in a little butter and sprinkle thyme over them. Combine the risotto, peppers and char and check for seasoning.

TUSCAN MUFFINS

2¾ cups all-purpose flour
¼ cup whole-wheat flour
1 package dry yeast
1 tsp. salt

In a medium-sized bowl, mix one cup of the all-purpose flour with the yeast and add enough warm water (not hot water) to make a moist and cohesive ball. Fill the bowl with enough warm water so the ball is covered. Let sit 5 to 15 minutes until the ball pops to the surface. Meanwhile take the remaining flours and put on top of the counter. Make a trench in the middle of the pile and add the salt. You will need to add water, a few tablespoons at a time, to the pile fluffing it into the flour with your fingers. The mixture should be slightly cohesive but not wet, as the yeast/flour ball will be quite wet. When the ball has risen to the surface of the water scoop it out and gather the two doughs together into one cohesive ball, kneading as little as possible. When they are altogether and well blended, roll the ball into a cylinder about 2″ in diameter. With a sharp knife cut off muffins about ½″ to ¾″ thick. Dust both sides with flour and set on a baking sheet. Each muffin should be several inches from the next. Cook in a preheated oven of 400° till they are golden brown and hollow sounding to the tap (about 20 minutes). Let cool on racks and serve with unsalted butter. They are quite dense, but marvelous tasting.

APRICOT CRÈME BRULÉE

8-10 dried apricots
  1 cup apple juice
  6 eggs
  5 tbsp. sugar
  3 cups heavy cream
  1 tbsp. vanilla extract
  ½ cup light brown sugar

In a small heavy-bottomed saucepan cover apricots with just enough apple juice to cover the tops; use good apple juice. Bring to a low simmer and cook with a lid until the apricots become very soft and mushy. Let cool and purée in a food processor. Separate the eggs and combine the yolks well with the white sugar and cream. Heat the mixture until very warm over a medium heat stirring constantly. Remove from the flame and add the vanilla. Spread apricot purée on bottom of baking dish. Then pour cream mixture through a stainer over the apricots. Put the dish into a roasting pan and surround it with an inch or so of boiling water. Bake it in a preheated oven at 300° for 25 minutes or until the custard is just setting around the edges but is still soft around the middle. Remove from the oven and let sit in the water bath until cool. Then refrigerate the custard for at least two hours or overnight. Just before serving sprinkle the custard with the brown sugar and put under a very hot broiler for a few seconds. If you cannot get your broiler hot enough, put the dish in cracked ice so the custard won't overcook while the brown sugar forms a nice hard crust.

**Steamed White Fish
Squash, Broccoli, and Turnips in Wine
Orange Oranges**

Serves four

STEAMED WHITE FISH

3-4 lbs. white fish fillets
1 cup raspberry vinegar
1 handful white peppercorns

Simmer the peppercorns together with the vinegar for about 10 to 15 minutes. Place a steamer rack over the vinegar and lay the fillets on top. Simmer for about 15 minutes.

SQUASH, BROCCOLI, AND TURNIPS IN WINE

2 yellow squash, sliced in ¼"
   round slices
1 head broccoli, cut into florets
3-4 white turnips, peeled and cut
   into slices ⅛" thick
⅔ cup wine (white or red)
   A few basil leaves for the wine
   and fresh chopped basil for
   the squash
   A pinch of thyme and a few
   crushed fennel seeds
1 cup water

If you have a tiered steamer use it with the turnips on the bottom and squash on the top as the squash takes the least time to cook. Just before done add the basil to the squash. Steam till just tender. Arrange on a platter or plates. Season, but use salt and pepper with discretion. You may want to use soy sauce for more flavor.

ORANGE ORANGES

             4 navel oranges
             2 cups sugar
             1 cup water
             1 tsp. lemon juice
             3 tbsp. Grand Marnier

With a vegetable peeler remove the orange part only of the skin from 2 oranges. Julienne into matchstick size pieces. Blanch in boiling water for 5 to 7 minutes and then rinse in cold water. Dry the orange rind with paper towels and let sit in the Grand Marnier. With a large sharp knife cut off both ends of all four oranges. Both ends means the rind and the white pith exposing the flesh. Stand them on end and remove all the peel and pith leaving the naked oranges. Then slice into ¼″ slices and arrange on a platter slightly overlapping or on individual plates. Sprinkle with additional Grand Marnier.

Slowly bring to a boil sugar, water and lemon juice. Cook until 245°, at the hard ball stage. Stir a few tablespoons into the orange peel. With the remaining syrup, one spoon at a time, glaze the orange slices. Chill this for several hours and serve with the sugared rinds which you have drained.

Walleye and Pike

I
t has been said that necessity is the mother of invention. It is also the mother of some terrific meals.

We were visiting our friends, Dave and Kim, who run a fish camp in the Bristol Bay region of Alaska. Dave and Ed were flying the last two guests into Dillingham and were to pick up supplies for the next couple of days. Kim and I had the luxury of lolling about camp for the few hours they were to be gone. We talked a lot about cooking, what it was like to cook every day for a camp full of fishermen, what problems were unique to cooking in the bush, what were some of her fish recipes. The talk was fun, but the two hours the men were supposed to be gone were stretching into three. Kim had wanted to get dinner cooking but needed the supplies to do so. The in-the-bush game of trying to hear the airplane's motor first was beginning to grow old with mirages of noises building, then destroying expectations. At long last the engine of Dave's Beaver could truly be heard, it was quite late but the daylight hours were still long in Alaska. The tardiness excuses were made and we waited for the supplies to be brought in. What, no groceries? There was then a very quiet "discussion" between Dave and Kim. "I gave you a grocery list!" "No you did not!" It, of course, didn't really matter who was supposed to give what to whom or who had lost what, the deed was done. (I am happy to report to all the ladies in the audience that the next day when I was fishing with Dave he was searching in his pockets for a twist-on and found the slip of paper he had so heartily denied having had the night before.) We were now faced with nothing to eat for dinner and the nearest restaurant or grocery store many hundreds of miles away. Ah, but we had a river full of fish lying before us.

We were obliged with a wonderful pike. Kim made Pike Puffs, her own great tempura-like concoction that quickly became nearly my favorite fish recipe that she does. Dinner was spectacular.

Rarely am I truly hundreds of miles away from the nearest grocery store. But there are times with the New England weather or my own fatigue that the grocery store might as well be a hundred miles away. I get the greatest pleasure out of figuring out what I can make from what's left in the pantry. It's a game of letting the imagination run wild, with certain restraints. It also is a game which has forced the creation of many a great recipe, and is terrific mental and culinary exercise for when the fisherman returns home not with the anticipated salmon, but with pike. Don't run for this cookbook, improvise!

Cool Vegetables with Herb Mayonnaise
Pike Couscous
Grilled Pineapple

Serves four

Some people don't know about couscous. It is a grain, similar to grits or rice, which comes from North Africa. It is a nice alternative and is delicious.

COOL VEGETABLES WITH HERB MAYONNAISE

As a first course, blanch a large variety of vegetables (broccoli, green beans, squash, carrots and cauliflower) and serve with a spiced or herb mayonnaise (see index for mayonnaise). This can be arranged on individual plates or presented as a centerpiece to be eaten with each person having their own bowls of mayonnaise.

PIKE COUSCOUS

       2 cups couscous
       2 cups chicken broth
       2 pounds pike fillets, skinned and
             cut into 2″ pieces
         Salt and pepper
       2 scallions, green part only,
             chopped
         Parsley, chopped finely
      ¼ tsp. cumin
      ¼ tsp. coriander, ground
       1 tsp. lemon rind, grated
      10 tbsp. unsalted butter

In a saucepan, bring the chicken broth to a boil adding 6 tablespoons butter, the ground cumin and coriander; add salt and pepper. Stir in the couscous, cover pan and remove from the heat and let stand for 5 minutes. In a fry pan sauté the fish and scallions in 3 to 4 tablespoons butter over medium-high heat for 4 minutes. Season with salt and pepper. Add the hot fish and scallions, parsley and lemon rind to the couscous. Toss well with a fork, fluffing up the couscous at the same time to break up any lumps. Taste for seasoning, adding more salt and pepper if necessary and serve in large soup plates.

GRILLED PINEAPPLE

       1 medium size ripe pineapple
       1 tbsp. brown sugar
       2 tbsp. Grand Marnier or
             Cointreau

Cut off the top, bottom and the sides of the pineapple with a large sharp knife. Remove the core and slice in thin slices, ¼″ thick or less. Grill until they start to brown. Sprinkle with the brown sugar and liqueur at the last minute and serve.

Sautéed Walleye with Noisette Butter and Shallots
Couscous
Broiled Tomatoes
Blancmange

Serves four

Broiled tomatoes are just that, slice them and run them under the broiler for a few minutes and season.

SAUTÉED WALLEYE WITH NOISETTE BUTTER AND SHALLOTS

2 lbs. fillets, dusted with flour
2-3 tbsp. unsalted butter
1 stick unsalted butter, cooked
    until noisette—see index
8 shallots, peeled and sliced thin

Cook the shallots in 1 tablespoon unsalted butter until they just start to turn a golden color and set aside. Sauté the fish in the butter and top with shallots and the noisette butter. Season with salt and pepper.

COUSCOUS

1 cup couscous
1 cup chicken stock
6-8 tbsp. unsalted butter
    Salt and pepper and a pinch
        cayenne
    Chopped parsley

In saucepan bring stock to a boil and add 4 tablespoons butter, salt and pepper and cayenne. When melted, stir in couscous and cover pan and let stand 5 minutes. Add 2-3 more tablespoons soft butter and let stand another minute covered. Then fluff the couscous with a fork and season well with salt and pepper and chopped parsley.

168

BLANCMANGE

1 cup whole milk
3 cups heavy cream
⅔ cup sugar
¼ tsp. salt
1 envelope gelatin with 1 tbsp.
   water
3 tbsp. Green chartreuse liqueur

Combine the gelatin and the water in a small custard cup. Set in a small frypan filled with hot water on low heat. This way the gelatin will melt without lumps. Combine milk and cream in a heavy bottom saucepan and scald. Remove from the heat and add the sugar, salt and stir to dissolve. Add the dissolved gelatin scraping the little custard cup well. Mix thoroughly by stirring and add 3 tablespoons green chartreuse. Pour blancmange into individual serving dishes and chill overnight.

Walleye *en Papillote*
Pasta with Parmesan and Romano Cheeses
Green Salad with Oil and Vinegar
Honey Dew Ice

Serves four

To use fresh grated cheeses in the pasta recipe is quite essential. Try not to cheat and use pre-grated, dried-up old stuff. Fresh pasta is also a nice touch, but I believe we are all getting quite tired of making it ourselves especially since it is possible to buy fresh pasta in the grocery store now. So unless the queen is coming to dinner or you've got a small child crazy to crank the pasta machine, buy this ready-made.

WALLEYE *EN PAPILLOTE*

1½-2 lbs. fillets
3 shallots chopped finely
4 sprigs tarragon
Rind of ½ an orange, with as little of the pith as possible, julienned and blanched
1 onion, sliced very thinly
4 tbsp. unsalted butter
⅔ cup white wine
Salt and pepper
Parchment paper

Sauté the onions and shallots in the butter until translucent and starting to brown. Season with salt and pepper and add wine. Reduce the mixture until it becomes syrupy. Add orange rind (12 pieces) and remove from heat. Cut 4 pieces of parchment paper into hearts, 12″ long and 10″ wide at the top (the widest part) and lightly butter. Divide fish onto the 4 pieces of parchment, setting the fish onto the right side of the heart. Divide up the onion, shallots, orange rind on top and top this with a nice size sprig of tarragon. Fold up heart. Bring the left side over to the right side and seal the edges with many little narrow folds to keep the heart closed. When you get to the tip, twist it tight and tuck it in. Bake on a baking sheet in a preheated 400° oven for 10 to 15 minutes. Put directly on plates and open each heart at the table. The aroma with the tarragon and orange rind will be delicious.

PASTA WITH PARMESAN AND ROMANO CHEESES

½ cup fresh grated Parmesan
  cheese
½ cup fresh grated romano cheese
  Salt and large cracked black
  pepper
6 tbsp. unsalted butter at room
  temperature
1 lb. fresh fettucini pasta

Cook pasta according to directions and drain. Toss with salt and pepper and butter, then cheeses. Serve at once.

Have a green salad of Boston and bibb lettuces with just oil, balsamic vinegar and salt and pepper.

HONEY DEW ICE

1 or 2 honey dew melons (you want
  about 3-4 lbs. of flesh)
3 tbsp. Midori liqueur or melon
  flavored liqueur
6-8 tbsp. confectioners' sugar
  Juice from 2 lemons
  A pinch of salt

Open the melon, discard the seeds, and purée the flesh in a food processor or blender. Add to the purée the remaining ingredients, tasting as you go to make sure the flavor is to your liking. Stir well, chill, taste again for flavor and balance. Make according to your ice cream machine's directions.

Pack the melon sorbet into parfait glasses and chill thoroughly. Garnish with mint sprigs or a strawberry cut and fanned out.

Crimped Walleye Steaks with Bernaise Sauce
Cabbage Patch Pasta Salad
Apple Tart

Serves four

For the Apple Tart, see page 125.

CRIMPED WALLEYE STEAKS WITH BERNAISE SAUCE

         4 steaks, 1⅓" thick
         1 bottle dry red wine
         ½ cup vinegar
       1½ qts. water
         1 tbsp. salt
       10 white peppercorns
         2 onions, chopped fine
         1 carrot, chopped fine
         3 shallots, chopped fine
         1 bay leaf
         1 tsp. dried thyme
  12-16 parsley stems
         3 tbsp. unsalted butter

Sauté the onions, carrot, and shallots in butter. Combine with the vinegar, wine, water, salt and peppercorns, bay leaf, thyme, and parsley stems and cook at a simmer for 30 minutes. Let cool. Now to cook the fish, bring the court bouillon to a violent boil. Arrange the fish steaks on a rack placed into the court bouillon and bring back to a boil; cover and remove pan from heat. Let sit 8-10 minutes. Drain, season with salt and pepper and serve with sauce.

BERNAISE SAUCE

¼ cup good wine vinegar
½ cup white wine
3 egg yolks
½ lb. unsalted butter, melted
1 tsp. fresh tarragon, chopped
3 medium shallots, chopped fine

1 tbsp. dried tarragon, revived in a
 little hot water
1 tbsp. chopped parsley
 Salt and fresh cracked or ground
 pepper

Bring the vinegar, wine, revived dried tarragon, parsley, salt and pepper to a boil. Reduce heat and on a low simmer, cook until reduced by ⅔ (this may be done ahead and refrigerated). Lower heat to the lowest and add yolks, one by one, whisking very fast. Remove from heat, add warm, melted butter very slowly and continue to whisk. Strain through coarse strainer into bowl and add fresh chopped tarragon and parsley. Taste for seasoning; if you need to add more salt, mix it first with boiling water to dissolve before adding.

CABBAGE PATCH PASTA SALAD

½ lb. cooked pasta
2 tbsp. toasted sesame oil
1 cup julienned savoy cabbage
2 red peppers, julienned
2 yellow peppers, julienned
2 cups snow peas, destrung and
   cut in half on the diagonal
 Corn oil for sautéing
½ cup olive or corn oil
2 tbsp. vinegar
1 tsp. prepared mustard
1 tsp. soy sauce
1 tbsp. fresh coriander
 Salt and pepper

After you've cooked the pasta, toss it with the sesame oil. Sauté the cabbage very briefly in a little corn oil. Sauté red and yellow peppers separately in corn oil until cooked, but still retain some crunch. Blanch, drain and dry the snow peas. Now make a dressing by zipping in the blender for a few seconds the vinegar, mustard, salt and pepper, soy sauce and chopped fresh coriander (if you can get it) and oil. Toss all ingredients together with the dressing and taste for seasoning.

Laura's Wild Mushroom and Potato Flan
Lemon-Lime Walleye
Green Salad
Drunk Melons

Serves four

The recipe for the Drunk Melons can be found on page 133. The recipe for the green salad can be found in your head or by perusing the "Basics" chapter in this book for a good vinaigrette that will go over fresh lettuce.

LAURA'S WILD MUSHROOM AND POTATO FLAN

8 oz. wild mushrooms cleaned, coarsely chopped (oyster mushrooms are good for this and readily available at many grocery stores)

2 tbsp. butter plus some for buttering the pan

⅔ cup cooked potatoes, coarsely chopped

Salt and pepper

3 whole eggs

2 egg yolks

1½ cups milk

½ cup cream

Pinch of thyme for the potatoes

Preheat the oven to 325°. Sauté the mushrooms in 2 tablespoons of butter. Season the cooked potatoes with salt, pepper, and a pinch of thyme. Have a kettle of boiling water ready. This recipe may be made in a 4-cup ring mold or in individual ½ cup capacity custard cups (use 8). Whichever is used, butter heavily with unsalted butter and set into a cake or roasting pan. Scald milk and cream. Cool a bit and slowly add to the whole eggs and yolks stirring constantly. Season well with salt and pepper and strain into a pitcher. Pour a bit into each mold. Divide the mushrooms and potatoes into each mold and add the rest of the custard. Pour the boiling water into the roasting pan around the edges so the mold(s) will have water coming ⅔ up the sides. Cover the large pan lightly with tinfoil and cook 15-20 minutes. A custard is a custard. Do not overcook. It will continue cooking after being removed from the heat. A knife inserted half way down should just barely be clean. Let sit 5 minutes in the mold(s) and unmold by running a knife around the edge. Garnish around the edge with sautéed watercress.

LEMON-LIME WALLEYE

2 lbs. walleye fillets
1½ sticks unsalted butter
    Grated rind of 2 limes, green
      part only
    Grated rind of 1 large lemon,
      yellow part only
1 garlic clove, very finely chopped
2 tsp. finely chopped parsley
    Salt and pepper

Whip butter till soft and fluffy. Add the rest of the ingredients, except the fillets. Season to taste. Mix well. Mound onto plastic wrap. Form into a cylinder. Freeze 24 hours and bring to room temperature before serving. Grill or broil the walleye, adding some of the compound butter just before finished cooking and then slather with more after cooking. Serve at once.

Shad, Catfish, and Smelt

S had and smelt are quite pretty little fish and when the run is on, fishing for them is truly an event. Clear, but long-ago, memories of fishermen at night ringing the shores of Lake Michigan with their torches and constant activity testify to the spectacle aspects of smelt fishing. Catfish are certainly as tasty as shad or smelt, but certainly are not as pretty. Catfish are quite ugly and the saying that the bravest man in history is the first man to have eaten a lobster, probably holds true for the first man to have eaten catfish too.

This is a problem, eating something that is ugly, particularly when you are involved in catching it, and preparing it. Once when we had just started teaching our very small children how to fish we made the mistake of catching a very ugly fish. We'd walked to the tidal brook near our house and fished off the bridge with close-faced reels and bait. Although it was very exciting when the line got heavier and we began to reel the fish in, to see this prehistoric thing which actually croaked at us on the end of the line; it is a wonder that our children ever wished to fish again. We did have the opportunity to teach them immediately about catch-and-release.

As the catfish will testify, the outside has nothing to do with the inside flavor. Really only in the case of an unknown species (as with the fish on the bridge) or with an obviously sick fish should ugliness be a deterrent to eating. This business of picking the parasites off the fish in order to get to the meat, although a closet practice, is something that is definitely disgusting and a waste of time. Yes, we know that the cooking will probably kill anything harmful, that restaurants are known to remove the parasites from the fish and serve it to the customer who is none the wiser, and that the parasites will not harm the meat once removed. But why do this? It's revolting and takes away the appetite. Even if we get someone else to remove the little bugger while we retire from the kitchen, we still know it was there, don't we? There are more fish in the sea, feel no guilt at tossing it out. We all take enough risk as it is eating commercially prepared foods. Why risk the good name of freshly caught, personally cared for, and healthy fish for the sake of one not too healthy fish? It surely is better to save a strong stomach for skinning a catfish than de-bugging a salmon.

**Fried Smelts with Noisette Butter
Fried Parsley
Grilled Pineapple with Strawberries**

Serves four

FRIED SMELTS

16-20 smelts (depending on size and
       appetite), cleaned with the
       heads off. There is no need to
       bone them as the bones are
       easily removed at the table.
  3 eggs
  2 tsp. corn oil, plus enough for
       deep-fat frying the fish
  2 tsp. water
    Salt and pepper
  1 cup flour
2½ cups bread crumbs
  2 tsp. thyme

In Imperial Rome these fish were cooked in a custard. We believe they are better fried. Combine the eggs, 2 teaspoons of corn oil, water and salt and pepper and set aside. Now make the bread crumbs by taking French or Italian bread cut into slices and drying them in the oven at 300°. Then reduce to crumbs in a food processor. Strain for uniformity of size and mix with the thyme. Rinse and dry smelts. Dredge in flour and shake off excess. Paint with egg mixture and roll in bread crumbs. Let rest on a cake cooling rack while the rest of the meal is prepared. They may be deep fried for about 1 minute (until golden) with the oil at 375° or you may fry them in an electric frying pan at 400°. In either case, after cooking drain on paper towels. They may be kept warm in the oven on racks.

NOISETTE BUTTER

2 sticks unsalted butter
1 tbsp. lemon juice

Cook the unsalted butter in a heavy bottomed saucepan constantly stirring until light brown. Remove from heat and let it continue to brown a bit more. (If it is browning too fast, pour the butter into another pan.) Stir in the lemon juice.

FRIED PARSLEY

1 large bunch parsley, washed and
dried very well

Deep fry the parsley in some corn oil in a heavy saucepan or sauté in some clarified butter until just crisp. Drain well on paper towels and sprinkle with salt just as you serve it.

GRILLED PINEAPPLE WITH STRAWBERRIES

1 medium-sized ripe pineapple
1 pint strawberries
1 tbsp. confectioners' sugar
2 tbsp. Grand Marnier or
Cointreau
Mint leaves

Cut off the top, bottom and the sides of the pineapple with a large sharp knife. Remove the core and slice in thin slices about ¼" thick or less. Grill until they start to brown and caramelize. Hull the strawberries and slice in half if large. Sprinkle with confectioners' sugar and Grand Marnier or Cointreau, toss and let sit several hours. To serve, place 4 slices of pineapple slightly overlapping on a plate and fill the center holes with the strawberries. Garnish with fresh mint if you can and be sure to provide fruit knives as well as forks, for the pineapple will be somewhat chewy.

The Best Catfish
Simple Green Salad
French Bread

Serves four

For a salad, you can invent one yourself, or refer to the "Basics" chapter in this book for an interesting vinaigrette. Use it on the most healthy looking greens you can find in the grocery store. French bread, of course, can be purchased successfully everywhere. But as anyone who has spent a little time in France knows, the fresher the better. It is easy to make yourself. Just use a white bread recipe and a French bread pan. Be sure to brush the crust several times in the cooking with cold water so a hard crust will form.

THE BEST CATFISH

1½-2 lbs. catfish fillets, cut into
         strips 1½" long and ½"-¾"
         wide
   ⅔ cup all-purpose flour
   ½ tsp. dried thyme
   ¼ tsp. salt
         A pinch of dried sage plus 1 tsp.
   ⅛ tsp. cayenne pepper
   4 grinds fresh black pepper
   2 boiling potatoes, peeled and cut
         into 1½"×½" pieces (keep in
         cold water)
   1 medium size eggplant, peeled
         and cut into 1½"×½" inch
         pieces, salted and left to drain
         in a colander 10 minutes
   5 tbsp. unsalted butter
   5 tbsp. corn oil
   2 garlic cloves, chopped fine
   1 tsp. grated lemon rind

Combine the flour with the thyme, salt, a pinch of sage, and both peppers. Dredge fish well in seasoned flour and shake off all excess. Let rest on cake cooling racks until ready to cook. The eggplant should now be rinsed, drained, dried and tossed in flour. In a heavy-bottomed skillet (2 pans at once is easiest), start with 1 tablespoon butter and 1 tablespoon of oil. Heat until sizzling and add catfish (not to be crowded) and sauté until browned. Set aside on warmed platter. Sauté eggplant and potatoes in separate pans until golden. Add together. Melt any remaining butter or use more, in empty pan and add the garlic. Sauté for 1 minute, then add 1 teaspoon dried sage and the catfish, eggplant and potatoes. Grate lemon peel over it all. Toss well and season to taste with salt and pepper.

Fried Catfish
Cole Slaw
Grits
Broiled Persimmons

Serves four

There is nothing so basic as catfish, or grits, or cole slaw. They are as basic as a hamburg, and just as easy to wreck. Care and attention should be paid to these recipes for the best results. All are delicious but dependent on being properly prepared.

FRIED CATFISH

2 lbs. catfish fillets, pat dry
2 eggs
   Flour for dusting
2 cups cornmeal, yellow or white
2 tsp. milk
2 tsp. oil
2 tsp. salt
½ tsp. fresh ground pepper
   Bacon fat
   Corn oil

Mix eggs, milk, oil, salt and pepper. Season fish very lightly with salt and pepper. Dust fish with flour. Paint with egg mixture and roll in cornmeal. Let rest on cake cooling racks until ready to cook. In heavy skillet, melt a combination of bacon fat and corn oil to ⅛" deep. When the oil is hot, fry fish until brown on one side and repeat for other side, but not quite as long.

COLE SLAW

Deli-bought, your mom's recipe, or see page 211.

GRITS

¾ cup grits
3 cups boiling water with 1½
    chicken bouillon cubes added
    to it. (Knorr is a good brand)
2 eggs
4 tbsp. unsalted butter, sliced
⅛ tsp. cayenne and a few grinds
    fresh pepper
½ lb. grated gruyére or sharp
    cheddar

Bring water and bouillon cubes to a boil and add butter, cayenne and fresh pepper. Then add grits. Cook, stirring over medium heat until the mixture thickens and becomes the consistency of oatmeal. Remove from heat and let cool slightly. Add eggs one at a time, stirring quickly to incorporate each one and then add cheese. Mix well and check for seasoning. Cook in a 350° preheated oven for 1 hour.

BROILED PERSIMMONS

4 persimmons—not too ripe
4 tbsp. unsalted butter
2 tsp. sugar
  Sherry

Cut persimmons in half. Broil till warm. Remove seeds and top each half with butter and sugar. Return to broiler and cook till butter is melted. Sprinkle with sherry and serve.

Sorrel Soup
Shad Roe
Pink New Boiled Potatoes
Rhubarb Fool

Serves four

SORREL SOUP

6 shallots, finely chopped
6 tbsp. unsalted butter
4 cups sorrel, clean and coarsely
    chopped
4 tbsp. flour
1 quart hot chicken stock
½ tsp. salt
2 cups heavy cream
  A squeeze of lemon juice
  Fresh ground pepper

Sorrel is one of the first things up in the garden. Sauté shallots in 2 tablespoons of the butter until soft and transparent. Add sorrel. Stir once or twice. Lower heat and cover and cook until the sorrel has completely wilted. Add chicken stock and salt and pepper. Simmer gently about 15 minutes. Blend in processor. Melt the 4 tablespoons of butter. When sizzling add the flour. Cook on medium heat for 4 minutes, stirring constantly. Take off the heat and add the hot stock mixture. Pour in about a cup, whisk to mix then add the rest, stirring. Bring back to a simmer. Remove from heat and add heavy cream and chill. Before serving, adjust to taste with salt and pepper and lemon juice.

SHAD ROE

    4 sets of roe
       Flour for dredging
       Salt and pepper
    4 tbsp. unsalted butter

Wash 4 sets of roe. Do not separate the sets unless they are already separated and if the roe are large you will need less. Remove clots, etc. Gently parboil if you like for about 4 minutes to toughen the outer membrane a little so it is less apt to burst. Let cool and then roll in flour seasoned with salt and pepper. Sauté 4-5 minutes per side in the butter. Serve with lemon wedges.

SHAD

If you are going to eat the shad, serve it with a white butter sauce. Try to get someone else to bone it, as it is very difficult. Salt and pepper each side of the fish. Spread with soft butter and squeeze the fish back together and broil it 6 minutes per side.

PINK NEW BOILED POTATOES

    3 per person
    1 stick unsalted, softened butter
    1 tsp. chopped chives
       Salt and pepper

Combine the softened butter with the salt, pepper and chives. Boil the potatoes for about 20 minutes. Drain and crack open. Spread with the butter mixture.

RHUBARB FOOL

  3 lbs. young rhubarb
  1 cup sugar
      Zest of 1 lemon, grated
1½ tsp. vanilla extract
 ¼ tsp. ground cloves
  2 cups heavy cream
  2 tsp. confectioners' sugar

Peel the rhubarb using a sharp knife. There is an almost transparent outside skin which comes off very easily. Then slice into very thin slices. This is most easily done when the rhubarb is held bunched together. In a heavy saucepan with a lid, put the rhubarb and the sugar and cover tightly and cook over low heat for 10-15 minutes. Remove the lid and raise heat and cook until excess liquid has evaporated, stirring constantly. It will become thick like applesauce. Be sure to stir it or the rhubarb will scorch. When ready, remove from the heat and add lemon zest and vanilla and set aside to cool. Whip the cream with the confectioners' sugar and the ground cloves until stiff. Fold the rhubarb in gently and chill.

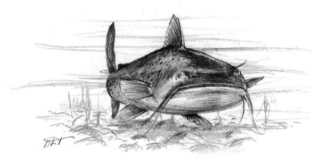

Bass and Panfish

We sure have tried a lot of methods for preserving fish. We've tried freezing the fish whole, we've tried freezing the fish just cleaned, we've tried freezing the fish fillets or steaks. We've tried smoked fish and we've tried dried and salted fish, we've tried canned fish. Ted was kind enough to make a presentation one time of some beautiful yellow perch which he had handily frozen whole in a wax milk carton filled with water. The perch were delicious, but I fear his preservation technique may be dying out with the innovation of plastic milk cartons.

One time when we were fishing for Atlantic salmon we caught more than anticipated and had to commandeer styrofoam fishing boxes from an abandoned fishing camp and pack them with Arctic snow. The merits of this procedure were in question until we put it inadvertently to the test. The bush pilot forgot to show up for a day or two and we missed the weekly train. There was quite a bit of Arctic slush oozing out of the boxes onto the carousel of Air Canada when we arrived in Boston and the condition of the fish was dubious. But miraculously the fish, which were then refrozen, were wonderful.

The relative merits of all these preservation techniques are difficult to assess. The reality is that they all impose on the fish certain taste elements which alter the fresh flavor of the fish. Smoked fish does not taste like fresh fish, nor does frozen fish. This is not to say that frozen fish is bad, it is simply different. And those differences vary in value; to some people frozen fish is worthwhile and to others not so, depending on taste, of course.

189

Some fish, I do believe, stand up better to freezing or smoking or salting or canning than do others. Certainly the salmon are the most resilient of all fish to any preservation method you can think of, as is evidenced by the Air Canada salmon. And fish you've never tasted fresh. If you've never tasted a fish fresh before, what have you to compare it to when you eat it smoked or salted for the first time? This was true of the yellow perch Ted gave us. Indeed they were good, but I didn't know till some time later how good they could really be.

One thing is for certain, the species of fish in this chapter are my five top candidates for which avoidance of freezing, smoking, salting, or canning remains sound advice. These fish are plentiful, relatively easy to catch, are well distributed geographically, and are the very best when eaten fresh.

Chicken Consommé
Almond Butter Smallmouth Bass
Sautéed Tomatoes
Fried Bread
The Pretty Easy Dessert

Serves four

CHICKEN CONSOMMÉ

1 bunch watercress, just the leaves
8 cups clear chicken broth (If you
    do not have homemade, use
    the least salty canned you can
    find.)
1 small onion, thinly sliced
3 carrots, peeled and chopped
    small
1 stick celery, chopped small
1 tbsp. unsalted butter

Sauté the onion, carrots, and celery in the unsalted butter over medium low heat until the onion is translucent. Then add the hot broth, bring to a boil and simmer for 30 to 40 minutes. Strain carefully. Keep hot. When ready to serve, divide the watercress leaves into each soup plate and add the hot broth.

ALMOND BUTTER SMALLMOUTH BASS

2 lbs. skinned bass fillets, broiled
1½ sticks butter unsalted and room
     temperature plus 2-3 tbsp. for
     frying the fish
¼ cup (approximately 2 oz.) whole
     almonds
   Salt and pepper
2 tsp. finely chopped parsley
½ tsp. grated orange rind

Make the compound butter 24 hours ahead by placing on a cookie sheet and toasting the almonds in a 300° oven until they turn a light beige. Remove from oven and cool. When completely cool, put in blender or food processor and blend until they become powder. Whip the butter until soft and fluffy. Add the powdered almonds, parsley, orange rind, and salt and pepper and mix well. Taste for seasoning. Then mound onto plastic wrap. Roll into a cylinder and pop into the freezer. Bring to refrigerator or to room temperature a few hours before serving time. Place pats of butter on broiled bass and serve.

SAUTÉED TOMATOES

4 large tomatoes—ripe and tasty
2-3 tbsp. good olive oil
    Salt and freshly cracked pepper
    Chopped parsley or thyme

Dip the tomatoes one by one in boiling water. Count to 10 and then dip in ice water. Peel, cut in half, scoop out seeds, remove core, and let drain for 10 minutes. Heat olive oil until water drops sizzle. Add tomatoes cut-side down and cook until juices start evaporating and the bottom browns. Turn and finish. Serve cut-side up, sprinkled with salt and pepper and the parsley and/or thyme.

NOTE: If the tomatoes are too huge, which homegrown ones can be indeed, then cut them in thick slices.

FRIED BREAD

½ loaf French bread
½ cup (1 stick) unsalted butter
2 tbsp. fontina cheese, grated, or
    any cheese
    Salt and pepper

Slice the French bread into 12 ½" pieces and dry them on a cookie sheet in a 300° oven. Do not let them cook. If you wish, rub one side of the bread with a garlic clove. In a heavy-bottomed sauce pan, melt the stick of butter till it sizzles. Put in the bread and brown both sides. Sprinkle with salt, pepper and cheese and put back in the oven just till the cheese melts.

THE PRETTY EASY DESSERT

There are several commercial water ices that are quite nice. Take 1 or 2 flavors and pack them into a mold, one inside the other and serve with berries or fruit sprinkled with liqueur. For example: raspberries with framboise or peaches with Grand Marnier. Place on the platter around the edge. To unmold ice cream, cover mold for a few seconds with a hot, wet towel. The ice cream should just slip out. Place in the middle of the fruit.

Little Fried Perch
Cucumber and Tomato Slices with Basil Vinaigrette
Rosemary's New Potatoes

Serves four

There is a difference in potatoes. In general, the smaller, thinner skinned potatoes are sweeter and need less cooking. The bigger and thick skinned potatoes are good for baking. Potatoes should be purchased according to how you plan to cook them, not according to whether you caught the fish in Idaho or Maine.

LITTLE FRIED PERCH

2 or 3 fish per person
2-3 cups milk
4 tbsp. oil
Flour for dredging
Parsley bunches
Lemon wedges
Salt and pepper

Gut the small fish with a sharp knife using the point. Wash them. Dry them and soak in a little milk for 10 minutes. Drain. Roll in flour and fry in very hot oil for 4 minutes. Set on paper towels to drain. Fry some bunches of parsley. Drain. Sprinkle fish with salt and pepper. Serve immediately with lemon wedges.

CUCUMBER AND TOMATO SLICES WITH BASIL VINAIGRETTE

2 tomatoes washed, peeled and
  sliced
2 cucumbers, washed and sliced
½ cup oil
½ tsp. prepared mustard
2 tbsp. vinegar
1 tsp. basil, fresh or revived in a
  little hot water
Salt and pepper

After slicing the cukes and tomatoes, arrange attractively on a platter. Now zip the remaining ingredients in the blender. Check the vinaigrette and adjust to suit your taste. Dribble over the tomatoes and cucumbers.

ROSEMARY'S NEW POTATOES

3 new potatoes per person
1 tbsp. fresh rosemary
2 tbsp. melted butter
Salt and pepper

Steam or boil the new potatoes. Sprinkle with rosemary, melted butter, and salt and pepper.

Perch Fillets
Bay Potatoes
Sliced Tomatoes
Fruit

Serves four

PERCH FILLETS

8-12 perch fillets
      Flour for dusting
1½ sticks plus 4 tbsp. unsalted
      butter
  4 shallots finely chopped and
      sautéed till translucent
  2 tbsp. tarragon, finely chopped
  1 tsp. Worcestershire sauce
      Salt and pepper

Whip 1½ sticks of butter till soft and fluffy. Sauté the shallots till translucent. Combine the shallots, whipped butter, tarragon, Worcestershire, and
salt and pepper and mix well and season to taste. Mound onto plastic wrap.
Shape into a cylinder and freeze 24 hours. Bring to room temperature before
using. Dust the perch with flour and sauté in hot, sweet butter. Serve with
pats of compound butter on top.

BAY POTATOES

1½ lbs. white boiling potatoes
    peeled and whole
½ cup red wine vinegar
4-5 dried bay leaves coarsely
    chopped
3 garlic cloves, medium-sized and
    coarsely chopped
¾ cup olive oil (good quality)
1½ tbsp. chopped parsley
    Salt and pepper
    Balsamic vinegar

Bring a large saucepan of water to a boil, add the vinegar and some salt. Drop in the potatoes, reduce heat to a simmer and cook till potatoes are done but firm. Drain and when cool enough to handle, cut into 1″ pieces; heat the olive oil, add the garlic and the bay leaves; bring to a simmer and lower the heat to the lowest and cook for 15 to 20 minutes. Remove the bay leaves and discard. Mash the garlic and return it to the warm oil. Pour over the potatoes. Toss, add a little balsamic vinegar, salt and pepper, chopped parsley and toss again.

Red, White and Green Largemouth Bass
Fried Tomato Slices
Fried Bread
Poached Peaches with Raspberries

Serves four

RED, WHITE AND GREEN LARGEMOUTH BASS

2 lbs. fillets
1 small white onion, roughly
    chopped
1 small red onion, roughly
    chopped
1 fresh green scallion, chopped
    into ½" pieces
  Olive oil
  Salt and pepper
1 tbsp. unsalted butter
1 tbsp. parsley, chopped fine

Sauté the white and red onions in butter until the white is translucent. Add scallion and cook for a few minutes more. Add parsley and stir and set aside. Baste fish with oil and sprinkle with salt and pepper. Broil until golden. Heat onions and season with salt and pepper and serve on top of the fish. Pour any juices from the pan over the fish.

FRIED TOMATO SLICES

4-6 ripe but firm tomatoes
1 egg, lightly beaten
   Pinch of thyme
   Salt and pepper
1 cup fine bread crumbs
   Unsalted butter

Slice the tomatoes ¼″ thick. Sprinkle the beaten egg with salt, pepper and a pinch of thyme. Dip each tomato slice first into the egg mixture and then into the bread crumbs. In a heavy skillet melt the butter until sizzling and then add the tomatoes and brown on both sides. Serve at once.

POACHED PEACHES WITH RASPBERRIES

4 perfect peaches, big ones
1 vanilla bean, split down the
   middle
2 cups sugar plus 2 tbsp. for
   sprinkling
4 cups water
1 tsp. lemon juice
1 qt. fresh raspberries
   Framboise

Slowly bring the water, sugar, lemon juice, and vanilla bean to a boil. Simmer 5 to 10 minutes. Add the peaches unpeeled. Return the syrup to a simmer and let cook about 5 to 8 minutes. Remove peaches to a rack and let cool. Peel when still slightly warm and then chill. Sprinkle the raspberries with a couple tablespoons of sugar and framboise. Let stand for one hour and then add the peaches and serve.

Smallmouth Bass Tempura
White Rice
Sake and Tea
Fortune Cookies

Serves four

You know how to make the rice and you can serve sushi as a first course if you are so inclined.

Choice of vegetables varies with the season.

SPRING LIST:	FALL LIST:
asparagus	sweet potato
zucchini	zucchini
carrots	carrots
broccoli	broccoli

SMALLMOUTH BASS TEMPURA

    3-4 lbs. bass, in bite-sized pieces
      2 egg yolks
    1⅔ cups ice water
    1⅔ cups sifted flour
      1 bottle of vegetable oil
         Vegetables

    Cut all the vegetables into pieces ½"×⅛"×2". Soak potatoes first in cold water for 15 minutes. Drain, dry and then use. Preheat oil to medium frying temperature, about 340°. Prepare batter. Lightly beat egg yolks. With the ice water in a large bowl, dump the flour in all at once. Stir a few times only. The batter should be gloppy and have the appearance of being only half-mixed. Dip vegetables and fish in flour first. Shake off excess and then mix gently in the batter only to cover and only a few at a time. Fry only a few at a time. Raise temperature slightly for cooking the fish. Let drain on paper towels; serve at once with dipping sauces. A variety of these sauces can be found at many gourmet shops and fancy supermarkets. You will want a soy sauce of some sort; keep to the Japanese types if you can. Mix a little grated ginger with the soy if you like. "Ponzu" is a good soy-type sauce with citrus juices, rice vinegar, malt and wheat.

————————————————

Sunfish on a Stick
Chocolate Chip Cookies

Serves four

This is a nice menu for your son to have in his pocket when he goes on his first solo fishing trip.

SUNFISH ON A STICK

4 little sunfish, pumpkinseeds, or
     crappies, cleaned
4 tbsp. hot bacon fat
½ cup corn meal
   Salt and pepper

Sprinkle the cleaned fish with salt and pepper. Dip each fish in corn meal and baste with hot bacon fat. Cook on a stick over the fire until the fish are crispy. If those who volunteered to be stick holders have returned to the fishing hole, you may also pan-fry these fish. After dipping the fish in corn meal melt 2 tablespoons bacon fat and 2 tablespoons unsalted butter in a pan and fry skin and all.

CHOCOLATE CHIP COOKIES

Use the Nestlé's Toll House cookie recipe and add an additional 2 tablespoons of white sugar (for the 6 oz. size bag of chocolate morsels) and omit nuts. The result is a thin cookie that is crunchy and just a bit chewy.

Basics

S ince cooking is very involved with lifestyle, this cookbook is truly a re-
flection of my style of life. I am a fisherman and a cook and cannot
separate that, which is why this book contains only recipes for fish that are
part of a fisherman's lifestyle. Nor do I wish to make a separation, for each
enhances the other, and perhaps dictates to the other occasionally, too. The
simplicity of the recipes and menus in this book presumes this combination.
I want my recipes simple enough so I can spend the day fishing. I always
will prefer a grilling technique for fish; it's quick and makes the fish taste
perfect. Yet I will not deny my love of cooking and so will use imagination
and variation in the menu combinations or in a specific dessert or vegetable
rather than on the fish.

This simplicity of lifestyle, in both cooking and fishing, seems compatible with the fashion, too. Right now the movement is away from gluttony,
both in the amount you fish for and the amount you eat. Many years ago
now, I can remember a foggy day on Nantucket with Mace and Ted and
Knowles and Ed. Mace and I were relegated to the house with tiny babies
and the others went fishing in our new Whaler. I'll never forget the car
pulling into the driveway with the boat trailered behind it and the snapper
blues pouring out of the cooler and live-well and splashing onto the decks of
the boat. We cleaned and foil-wrapped until two in the morning. What a lot
of work! There are still many bluefish to be had, but I think Ed and Ted
would now find some way to better control Knowles and themselves—I
think.

I used to wonder when I was a child why I had to clean my plate because there were starving children in China. How were the Chinese children
going to get what was left on my plate? This resistance to the adult's guilt
trip has stood me well in later years when the fashion has gone to eating
less, more simply and staying thin. Eating fish is extremely good for you and
has far fewer calories than meat. It is thought now that it even aids in pre-
venting cancer. I have tried in this book not to erode the natural goodness or
limited caloric content of fish by including a lot of heavy sauces and gooey
desserts in the menus. These really aren't very compatible with fish. Fashion has complimented my lifestyle and affected this book in one other re-
gard. Remember the days when Dad sat down to a meal and, anticipating

207

meat, potatoes, vegetables, and dessert, would question the solvency of his marriage if he was presented with just two items on his plate? Now real men will eat just quiche and salad for Sunday's supper. I believe menus have finally gotten away from the four-item syndrome and are free to accommodate the situation and appetite.

The fisherman in me has definitely added a sense of respect for the fish in both my fishing and my cooking. I put the ones back that I do not intend to eat. I try to keep the fish cooled down from the minute he is killed till he is cooked. The sharpest knives are used and the greatest care taken in cleaning him. And the menus here presumed a certain level of concentration and respect for their preparation. It may seem in many cases that you must resemble a short-order cook to assemble these menus. Cooking everything at once and demanding that it all come to the table at the same time and remain hot requires the kind of focus on cooking that I relish. This may mean the second martini must sit untouched in the living room with the guests. But the results of such concentration in the kitchen can produce such a nice event at the table the guests surely will forgive you your absence from them. It is true that pre-preparation of some of the basics can make a meal with guests less hectic. Also just having some basic items in the freezer or refrigerator can make the smallmouth bass that suddenly appears for dinner that much more exciting. Making a batch of basil compound butter and freezing it just as the basil comes into your garden, or making extra home-made mayonnaise when you're throwing together a chicken salad are good habits.

Just as Mr. Fish has given you the ultimate in fishing and cooking pleasure, it is truly wonderful to be able to pass along some of that pleasure to guests or family. Spend the time and do it right. Advance preparation is one of the keys to fine cooking. To have on hand ingredients that can take an ordinary meal and make it a gourmet meal is straight-forward smart. But to also spend a small amount of time and effort to prepare some basic items, such as homemade mayonnaise or vinaigrette, so they are on hand also, can begin to push you into the category of a fine cook.

When we were in Alaska last we heard about a dish that the Eskimos prepare and have on hand well in advance. It is called "stinky heads." In plastic gallon drums that had previously held the winter's supply of cooking oil they gather the heads of all the salmon they can find and close the bucket and bury it for a couple of weeks. They open it and eat the "stinky heads" when they really smell the fish odor permeating from the ground. This chapter is not suggesting preparation of "stinky heads." (As the Eskimo woman said, "Stinky heads make your stomach growl.") Listed below are just some nice benign things you should know how to make and have on hand.

RISOTTO

2 onions, chopped very fine
4 oz. unsalted butter or a mixture
    of butter and olive oil
1½ cups Italian arborio rice
4-5 cups hot fluid, either stock or
    water or a combination of both

In a heavy-bottomed, wide saucepan, heat butter. Sauté onions until translucent. Add rice. Cook, stirring until it becomes very white, shiny and very hot to touch. Then, over medium–high heat, add only enough stock so that the rice is just covered. Holding the handle of the saucepan, firmly swish the rice around and around. Do this every 2-3 minutes, keeping a low simmer going in the pot in between. This is so the rice won't stick. (If you weaken and stir the rice, then you must continue to stir until done.) As soon as you can distinguish the grains of rice again, then add another ½ cup of fluid. Keep swirling the pot and adding more fluid as it becomes absorbed. Taste when you feel it is nearly finished. It should be firm to the bite, with a tender, creamy texture—not too dry and not too runny. Season with salt and pepper. If using saffron powder, dissolve in hot broth or water and add halfway through, or later, depending on how strong a saffron taste you desire. The nearer the end it is added, the stronger the taste. Parmesan and extra butter can be added at the end of cooking.

OLIVE BASTING OIL

1 cup good olive oil
8 peeled garlic cloves
1½ tsp. thyme
1 bay leaf

Heat on low heat all the ingredients for 20-30 minutes. Remove garlic and keep to spread on toast or mash and put in mayonnaise.

MAYONNAISE

      3 egg yolks
      ¼ cup vinegar or lemon juice
      2 tsp. mustard prepared
      ½ tsp. salt
      ¼ tsp. ground pepper
      1 dash cayenne
      2 cups oil—corn or good olive

In a bowl combine: vinegar or lemon juice, salt, mustard, pepper, cayenne. Let salt melt. Add egg yolks. Whisk until frothy and well combined. Add oil very slowly in a dribble until the mayonnaise seems to have started to take and thicken. Then you may add the oil faster. When finished, taste for seasoning and adjust with salt, pepper, mustard, and lemon juice or vinegar. Be sure to dissolve the salt in vinegar or water first as it will not dissolve well in the mayonnaise. Whisk in a tablespoon of hot, hot water to finish it. Any dry herbs added should first be revived in hot water or no flavor will exude through the oil which will coat them. This may also be done in the food processor with no fuss/no mess.

BREAD CRUMBS

You can use either fresh or dried French or Italian bread. If you need to dry the bread further, place slices on cookie sheets in a 300° oven until just hard. Break into pieces and blend in the food processor with the steel blade until fine. Then shake through a strainer. The bread crumbs that result are all of an even size and will give a better texture when cooked.

BASIC VINAIGRETTE

      2 tbsp. vinegar
      ½ cup good olive oil
      1 tsp. prepared mustard
         Salt and pepper
         Herbs of your choice

Combine all ingredients in a blender and zip on high for a second or two.

If you are trying to think of a good salad to have with your fish here are the ones in this book which might suit your meal, or at least spark an idea.

GREEN AND PURPLE COLE SLAW

        3 cups finely shredded green savoy
              cabbage
        3 cups finely shredded purple
              cabbage
        1 large carrot, grated
        ½ tsp. salt
        2 tsp. prepared mustard
        ¼ tsp. ground pepper
        1 dash cayenne
        3 egg yolks
        2 cups corn oil or good olive oil
        1 tsp. salt
        ¼ cup vinegar
        2 tsp. sugar
        ¼ cup sour cream
        2 tsp. lemon juice
        2 tsp. caraway seeds
        1 tbsp. dry mustard

Keep the cabbages separate. Divide the carrot between them.

Now make a mayonnaise by combining in a bowl: ½ teaspoon salt, the prepared mustard, pepper, and cayenne. Let the salt melt and add the egg yolks. Whisk until frothy and well combined. Add the oil slowly in a dribble until the mayonnaise begins to take and thicken. Then you may add the oil faster. When finished, taste for seasoning and adjust. Add a tablespoon of hot water to finish it off. This also can be made in a food processor. Now add the remaining ingredients to the mayonnaise and divide between the two cabbages. Be sure to dissolve the salt in vinegar first as it will not dissolve well in the mayonnaise. Mix well and taste for seasoning. You will want a nice sweet sour taste. Grate a little black pepper over each and chill for several hours. Mix again before serving.

PANZANELLA SALAD

  8 thick slices day-old Italian or
        French bread
½ cup stock
  3 tbsp. butter
  2 tomatoes peeled, seeded, and
        coarsely chopped
  1 medium cucumber, seeded and
        chopped
  1 small red onion, chopped
  1 head romaine lettuce
     A few bitter greens, such as
       chicory or escarole
     Shredded fresh basil leaves
     A good vinaigrette—your own,
       or see page 210
     Salt and pepper

Cut the bread into large cubes and dribble the stock over them. Fry in butter until crisp and let cool. Combine all remaining ingredients and toss with the vinaigrette. Check for salt and pepper and let sit a little before serving, to meld the flavors.

EGG AND ASPARAGUS SALAD

  2 hard-boiled eggs
½ lb. asparagus, peeled
  2 heads Boston lettuce, cleaned
        and dried
  1 tbsp. vinegar
  1 tsp. prepared mustard
½ cup olive oil
  1 tbsp. mayonnaise
     Salt and pepper

To hard-boil the eggs, set in cold water with a tablespoon of white vinegar, bring to a boil, reduce to a medium simmer and cook, using a timer, for 9 minutes. Then plunge in cold water. Peel, chop and set aside.

Steam the asparagus, cut into 1″ pieces and combine with the lettuce. Make a vinaigrette by combining in the blender the vinegar, mustard, oil and dashes of salt and pepper and blending for a second or two. Add the mayonnaise and motorize for another second. Toss the vinaigrette first with the asparagus and lettuce and then add chopped egg. Toss lightly, taste for salt and pepper and serve.

CHICORY SALAD

1 small head chicory
1 head Boston lettuce
1 small bunch watercress
6 slices medium crisp bacon, or
    better yet, pancetta

For the dressing:

3 tbsp. vinegar
  Salt and pepper
1 tsp. prepared mustard
1 tsp. tarragon, revived in a little
    hot water
1 very small clove garlic, mashed
    and then chopped very fine
¼ cup olive oil

Wash the greens carefully. Shake dry and roll up in clean terry towels. (This can be done several hours before using.) Combine all the ingredients for the dressing in a blender and blend on high. Toss salad with dressing. Add bacon or pancetta and then taste and adjust seasoning.

SALAD OF ZUCCHINI AND YELLOW SQUASH AND TOMATO

1 head Boston lettuce or 2 Bibb,
    cleaned
3 tiny yellow squash, julienned
2 tiny zucchini, julienned
1 tomato, skinned, seeded,
    drained and julienned
Corn oil or cooking oil

2 tbsp. good vinegar
  Salt and pepper
1 tsp. good prepared mustard
⅓ cup olive oil
  Fresh basil leaves—the little-
    leafed kind, if possible, called
    spiley globe

First mix salt and pepper and vinegar and then add the olive oil, mustard, and basil leaves and zip in the blender for a second or two. Sauté zucchini and yellow squash in corn oil until they just begin to cook. Be sure they keep some of their crispness. Let cool. Toss with lettuce, tomatoes and dressing. Taste for salt and pepper. Or you can keep the squashes separate and lay the alternate colors out in groups on top of the lettuce.

WATERCRESS SALAD

  1 bunch watercress without stems,
      washed
  2 Bibb or 1 head Boston lettuce,
      washed
 ½ head red lettuce, washed
  2 tbsp. wine vinegar
  1 tsp. prepared mustard
     Salt and pepper
  1 tsp. soy sauce
  1 garlic clove, peeled and crushed
 ⅓ cup good quality olive oil

Rub salad bowl with garlic. Combine in the blender the vinegar, mustard, soy sauce and salt and pepper and zip on high for a second or two. Add olive oil and blend again. Toss with the greens and serve with a crusty bread and butter and a couple of cheeses.

THREE GREEN SALAD

     At least three different greens;
      endive, watercress, Boston
      lettuce or what is available to
      you
  6 strips of cooked bacon
 ½ cup olive oil
  3 tbsp. wine vinegar
  2 tsp. good prepared mustard
  1 tbsp. mayonnaise
 ¼ tsp. garlic, chopped fine or
      squeezed through a press
     A dash of soy sauce
     Salt and pepper

Combine the vinegar, salt and pepper, mustard, garlic and soy sauce. Add the oil and mix well. Now add the mayonnaise and mix well again. Toss dressing with the greens. Crumble the bacon into the salad and toss again.

CHICORY AND ESCAROLE SALAD

1 small head escarole, washed
   and dried
1 small head chicory, washed
   and dried
1 head Boston lettuce, washed
   and dried
1 orange, in sections and cleaned
   of membranes
1 small shallot and 1 very small
   garlic clove, chopped extra
   fine
1 tbsp. vinegar
   Salt and pepper
   Grated rind of 1 orange
⅓ cup light olive oil
1 tbsp. heavy cream

Combine vinegar, salt and pepper, shallot and garlic. Let stand a bit to dissolve salt, then add oil, cream and orange rind. Mix well. Toss with lettuces and orange segments.

SALAD OF MELON, PEARS, AND CUCUMBERS

½ cup hazelnuts, toasted and
   chopped coarsely
4 pears
2 medium sized cucumbers
1 small melon
   Lemon juice
1 tsp. mustard
2 tbsp. red wine vinegar
½ cup hazelnut or walnut oil
   Salt and pepper

Combine the vinegar, mustard, oil and salt and pepper in the blender. Turn on high for a couple of seconds and then set aside. Toast the hazelnuts in the oven set at 300°. Remove and cover with a towel for 5 or 10 minutes, then rub off the skins and chop coarsely. Peel, core, and slice the pears and toss with a little lemon juice. Add slices of melon, about an equal amount to the pears. Peel, seed, and slice the cucumbers. Toss the cucumbers, pears and melon together with the vinaigrette and let sit an hour or so. Just before serving, toss in the toasted hazelnuts.

BIBB SALAD

4 heads Bibb lettuce, cleaned
A few snips of chive
2 tbsp. red wine vinegar
½ cup good olive oil
1 tsp. prepared mustard
Salt and pepper

Combine vinegar, oil, mustard, and salt and pepper in a blender and zip on high for a second or two. Toss with the lettuce and chives.

GREEN SALAD

1 head Boston, red, oakleaf lettuce
    or Bibb (no strong tastes)
1 tbsp. vinegar
1 tsp. prepared mustard
½ cup oil
1 tsp. basil
Salt and pepper

Blend all but the lettuce in the blender on high-speed. Toss with the lettuce.

CUCUMBER AND TOMATO SLICES WITH BASIL VINAIGRETTE

2 tomatoes, washed, peeled and
    sliced
2 cucumbers, washed and sliced
½ cup oil
½ tsp. prepared mustard
2 tbsp. vinegar
1 tsp. basil, fresh or revived in a
    little hot water
Salt and pepper

After slicing the cukes and tomatoes, arrange attractively on a platter. Now zip the remaining ingredients in the blender. Check the vinaigrette and adjust to suit your taste. Dribble over the tomatoes and cucumbers.

Index

This book was designed by DeCourcy Taylor Jr.
The type is Caslon 540 and was set by DEKR
    Corporation, Woburn, Massachusetts
The color separations were made by
    Uni·Graphic·Inc., Saugus, Massachusetts
The paper is Glatfelter Hi-Brite Offset
The printing and binding were by The Alpine
    Press, Inc., Stoughton, Massachusetts